Emancipatory and Participatory Research for Emerging Educational Researchers

Emancipatory and Participatory Research for Emerging Educational Researchers is a concise fundamental guide on two related models of education research—emancipatory and participatory.

In addition to providing an introduction to these research models, this book also studies them through the lens of critical practice as well as pure research and provides case studies as examples. It highlights a variety of data collection techniques that are used in education research, from visual methods to interviews, and the strategies that researchers apply to ensure the research process involves and benefits the participants.

Emancipatory and Participatory Research for Emerging Educational Researchers functions as a useful "how-to" guide for first-time and less experienced researchers. Furthermore, it highlights not only how participatory research is by its nature emancipatory but also the overlaps between the two models' approach to data collection.

Joe Barton attained his MRes from the University of Bath, UK. He has been involved in disability sport as both a sportsperson and a coach and now counsels young people with disabilities on career choices and development.

Simon Hayhoe is Reader in Education at the University of Bath, UK. He is also a center associate in the Centre for the Philosophy of Natural and Social Science at the London School of Economics, UK, and an associate of the Scottish Sensory Centre at the University of Edinburgh, UK.

Qualitative and Visual Methodologies in Educational Research
Series Editors: Rita Chawla-Duggan and Simon Hayhoe,
University of Bath, UK

We are increasingly living in an era where students and researchers are under severe time pressures, whilst the amount of research topics, methodologies, data collection methods and ethical questions continue to grow. The *Qualitative and Visual Methodologies in Educational Research* series provides concise, accessible texts that take account of the methodological issues that emerge out of researching educational issues. They are ideal reading for all those designing and implementing unfamiliar qualitative research methods, from undergraduates to the most experienced researchers.

Books in the series:

- Are compact, comprehensive works, to appeal to final year undergraduates and early career postgraduates, at masters and doctoral level—both PhD and EdD. These works can also be easily read and digested by emerging, early career researchers, or raise issues applicable to experienced researchers who are keeping up with their field.
- Reflect on a single methodological problem per volume. In particular, the titles examine data analysis, research design, access, sampling, ethics, the role of theory, and how fieldwork is experienced in real-time.
- Have chapters that discuss the context of education, teaching and learning, and so can include a psychological as well as social and cultural understanding of teaching and learning in non-traditional or non-formal, as well as formal settings.
- Include discussions that engage critically with ontological and epistemological debates underpinning the choice of qualitative or visual methodologies in educational research.

The *Qualitative and Visual Methodologies in Educational Research* series includes books which stimulate ideas and help the reader design important and insightful research that improves the lives of others though education, to ultimately inspire the development of qualitative and visual methodologies.

Titles in the series include

Emancipatory and Participatory Research for Emerging Educational Researchers
Theory and Case Studies of Research in Disabled Communities
Joe Barton and Simon Hayhoe

For more information about this series, please visit: https://www.routledge.com/Qualitative-and-Visual-Methodologies-in-Educational-Research/book-series/QVMER

Emancipatory and Participatory Research for Emerging Educational Researchers

Theory and Case Studies of Research in Disabled Communities

Joe Barton and Simon Hayhoe

LONDON AND NEW YORK

First published 2022
by Routledge
2 Park Square, Milton Park, Abingdon, Oxon OX14 4RN

and by Routledge
605 Third Avenue, New York, NY 10158

Routledge is an imprint of the Taylor & Francis Group, an informa business

© 2022 Joe Barton and Simon Hayhoe

The right of Joe Barton and Simon Hayhoe to be identified as authors of this work has been asserted in accordance with sections 77 and 78 of the Copyright, Designs and Patents Act 1988.

All rights reserved. No part of this book may be reprinted or reproduced or utilized in any form or by any electronic, mechanical, or other means, now known or hereafter invented, including photocopying and recording, or in any information storage or retrieval system, without permission in writing from the publishers.

Trademark notice: Product or corporate names may be trademarks or registered trademarks, and are used only for identification and explanation without intent to infringe.

British Library Cataloguing-in-Publication Data
A catalogue record for this book is available from the British Library

Library of Congress Cataloging-in-Publication Data
A catalog record for this book has been requested

ISBN: 978-0-367-53975-7 (hbk)
ISBN: 978-0-367-53976-4 (pbk)
ISBN: 978-1-003-08392-4 (ebk)

DOI: 10.4324/9781003083924

Typeset in Times New Roman
by Apex CoVantage, LLC

Contents

Acknowledgments viii
Biographies ix

1 Introduction 1

*The context of emancipatory paradigm and
   participatory methodology 1
From philosophy to paradigm 1
Critique of the emancipatory paradigm and a call
   for alternatives 3
A rundown of the chapters 4*

2 Emancipatory and participatory research 6

*Introduction 6
   Practice as paradigm and methodology 7
   Ethical considerations prior to designing
      emancipatory participatory research 10
   Bias, reflexivity, organizational impact,
      and research quality 12
   Intervention development and participant
      and participant observer satisfaction 13
Designing an emancipatory participatory study 15
   Recruitment procedures, informed consent,
      and participant information 15
   Participant inclusion and exclusion criteria 16
   From transcription to critical thematic or
      theory-based analysis 18*

3 Case study of a small-scale university-based postgraduate project 20

Introduction 20
   The context of disability in the university and what follows in this chapter 21
   Summary of the methodologies and methods 22
      Research methodologies 22
      Data collection methods 23
      Methods of data analysis and representation 25
   Findings that arose from the study 28
      Identity and impairments 28
      Disclosure and academic culture 30
      Support 33
   The issues that this study identified 35
      Ableism and constructions of disability 36
   Conclusion 38

4 Case study of a large-scale museums-based project 40
SIMON HAYHOE, HELENA GARCIA CARRISOZA, JONATHAN RIX, KIERON SHEEHY, AND JANE SEALE

Introduction 40
   The context of the project 41
   The development of the sessions 43
   The approach to using emancipatory participatory methodology 45
   The design of the methodology 45
   Data collection methods 46
   The findings from the participatory practice 48
      Intersubjective validity 48
      Contextual validity 51
      Participatory validity 52
      Catalytic validity 55
      Ethical validity 56
      Empathic validity 57
   Problems that arose through participation and the development of further validities 59
      Tensions caused during participatory practice 60
      A breakdown of the tensions that caused the problems 61

Concluding discussion—addressing the tensions within the group 64

5 Conclusion 67

References 70
Appendix 74
Index 76

Acknowledgments

We would like to thank all the participants in the projects that became the case studies in Chapters 3 and 4. We could not have written this without them. We would also like to acknowledge our families for their support during the research and writing of this book, particularly during the difficult days of the COVID-19 pandemic.

Biographies

Joe Barton attained his MRes from the University of Bath. He has been involved in disability sport since childhood, as both a sportsperson and as a coach, and he now counsels young people with disabilities on career choices and development.

Simon Hayhoe is Reader in Education at the University of Bath. He is also a center associate in the Centre for the Philosophy of Natural and Social Science, London School of Economics, and an associate of the Scottish Sensory Centre, University of Edinburgh. He was until recently a technical advisor to the World Health Organization. Simon's current work focuses on qualitative and visual methodologies, visual impairment and education, disability arts, access to cultural heritage, and accessible and inclusive technology.

Contributor Biographies (Chapter 4):

Helena Garcia Carrizosa is a research associate and PhD student at the Open University. From October 2016 to January 2020, she was a partner of the European Commission's ARCHES project. Before working for the Open University, she studied at the Courtauld Institute of Art and University College London and worked for the National Portrait Gallery.

Jonathan Rix is a professor of learning support at the Open University. His research interests focus on policies, practices, and language that facilitate inclusion within the mainstream; capturing diverse perspectives; and developing models to facilitate our thinking about the form and function of education. Professor Rix has a strong and broad interest in issues relating to learning difficulties and issues of equality and participation.

Kieron Sheehy is Professor of Education (Innovation Pedagogies) at the Open University. His research interests are within the broad field of inclusive education, often focusing on how teaching approaches or services can be developed to successfully support diverse groups of learners. Professor Sheehy supervises research within this area and has an interest in addressing issues for those who might be stigmatized and excluded within educational systems.

Jane Seale is Professor of Education at the Open University. She has developed a national and international profile in the field through key roles such as President of the Association for Learning Technology (2006–2007) and Digital Inclusion Consultant to the ESRC-funded Technology Enhanced Learning (TEL) Programme in the UK (2009–2012). Between 2007 and 2010, Professor Seale was Codirector of the ESRC National Centre for Research Methods. She has recently served on the Research Excellence Framework (REF) 2014 education panel in the UK that was responsible for assessing the quality of research conducted in UK universities.

1 Introduction

This book introduces the reader to a participatory paradigm and emancipatory methodology in educational research, a concept that is shortened to emancipatory participatory methodology throughout the book for brevity. The methodology discussed in this book is designed to develop educational projects that are informed by a disability studies approach, two examples of which are discussed in the case studies featured later in this book.

The models of participatory research practice featured in this book, what we refer to as "participatory practice" for brevity in the rest of the book, are contemporary methods designed to include stakeholders in the research process and dissemination. This methodology also allows participants to guide the forms of data collection used, the assessment of existing educational practices and technologies, and the evaluation of the research procedures.

As the emancipatory participatory methodology featured in this book was developed through an exploration of research traditions in disability studies, it is the first task of this book to show how these traditions were synthesized within the framework of disability studies and the study of disability within the social sciences.

The context of emancipatory paradigm and participatory methodology

From philosophy to paradigm

From its early years, the sociological discipline of disability studies has been entwined with the concepts of emancipation and participation. The Union of the Physically Impaired Against Segregation in the United Kingdom and the Independent Living Movement in the United States in particular established a political and theoretical impetus and lobbied academic researchers on issues pertaining to the lives of people with disabilities. This impetus resulted in the creation of the original British Social Model of Disability and

DOI: 10.4324/9781003083924-1

the widespread public lobbying of government and institutions for disability rights using professionally inspired investigations and evidence (Barnes and Mercer 2010).

Following this early social movement, contemporary writing on research, emancipation, and people with disabilities can arguably be traced to a special issue of the journal *Disability, Handicap & Society*, now known as *Disability & Society*, in 1992. This issue explored issues surrounding traditional philosophies of social studies and introduced Oliver's (1992) thesis that traditional research excluded people with disabilities and contributed to the wider oppression and exclusion of disabled communities. Consequently, Oliver called for a renegotiation of the nature of disability research and for the elaboration of an *emancipatory research framework*, in particular, that, if followed, would improve rather than restrict the lives of disabled communities.

Oliver's (1992) most important proposal for the renegotiation of research and the "emancipation" of people with disabilities was to insist on a rebalancing of power relations between the researcher and the researched. This process significantly involved realigning the role of participants in the design and planning process of a given study and putting the skills of researchers at the participants' disposal.

Following the advent of the emancipatory paradigm, and with the support of academics of disability studies and contemporary disability organizations, research projects that promote the voices and demands of people with disabilities have now proliferated since the new millennium (Barnes 2003). Furthermore, support for the emancipatory paradigm can be seen to be influenced by Priestley et al.'s (2010) exploration of organizations promoting the rights of people with disabilities in Europe.

Since 1992, there have also been multiple reviews of and alternating approaches to emancipatory research, requiring a clarification of terminology of the contemporary research processes. This book's approach follows Danieli and Woodham's (2005) in referring to Oliver's original philosophy of emancipatory research as an emancipatory paradigm to distinguish it from other forms of emancipatory research. In addition, the approach in this book also adopts Stone and Priestley's (1996) principles of emancipatory research as the *values* of its emancipatory model, including:

- The adoption of a social model of disability as the ontological and epistemological basis for research production
- The surrender of falsely-premised claims to objectivity through overt political commitment to the struggles of disabled people for self-emancipation
- The willingness only to undertake research where it will be of some practical benefit to the self-empowerment of disabled people and/or the removal of disabling barriers

Introduction 3

- The devolution of control over research production to ensure full accountability to disabled people and their organisations
- The ability to give voice to the personal while endeavouring to collectivise the commonality of disabling experiences and barriers and
- The willingness to adopt a plurality of methods for data collection and analysis in response to the changing needs of disabled people.

(Stone and Priestley 1996, p. 706)

Critique of the emancipatory paradigm and a call for alternatives

Despite what can arguably be called the success of the emancipatory paradigm, it has also faced criticism. For instance, Danieli and Woodhams (2005) called for alternative models to ensure that the emancipatory paradigm does not reach a state of hegemony and retains its paradigmatic diversity. In addition, aspects of the emancipatory paradigm have caused problems for researchers, including the need for the participants to self-identify as disabled and an absence of focus in contemporary organizations (Barnes 2003). Furthermore, other authors have witnessed disagreements between the participating parties over funding, ownership of research output, and expectations (Gustafson and Brunger 2014).

Furthermore, there has also been criticism of the emancipatory paradigm based on its requirement for emancipatory studies to rigidly adopt the perspectives and philosophies of the British Marxist social model of disability. For example, Shakespeare and Watson (2002) argue that having to adopt the ideological foundation of Oliver's social model limits the perspective of research and the range of interventions it can suggest.

The concerns raised that many of these problems were not successfully addressed on either a theoretical or practical level after their initial conception suggested that there was a need to understand the emancipatory paradigm better. However, within disability studies, the political convictions that underpinned the emancipatory paradigm remained worryingly unchallenged, and little evolution of thinking or practice was evident in the early years of the new millennium.

Subsequently, a branch of disability studies based on alternative forms of material philosophy proposed an alternative approach as the millennium progressed. For instance, both Coole (2015) and Pezdek and Rasiński (2017) identify the ideas of Kant and Foucault as providing philosophical bases for understanding emancipation through their discussion of the nature of power and the potential for freedom from it. For these theorists, the key text depicting Kant's (1991) perspective was *An Answer to the Question: "What Is Enlightenment,"* while Foucault engaged with the concept throughout his body of work (Tremain 2015).

4 Introduction

Both Kant and Foucault's notions of freedom are associated with a more active role for the individual rather than being emancipated by others, viewing it as "individual critical engagement with their own political, cultural and material circumstances" (Coole 2015, p. 533). The method through which this is achieved differs slightly between the two philosophers. For example, Kant's notion suggested that thought processes based on logic are central to such efforts, while Foucault required an awareness and conscious resistance to the specific ways in which societies influenced the thoughts of people within them (Coole 2015). Consequently, Foucault (1997) goes further in his concept of "domination," which he conceived of as situations where individuals can't emancipate themselves. Studies in the Foucauldian tradition within disability studies therefore position themselves in opposition to states of domination (Pezdek and Rasiński 2017; Tremain 2015).

Thus, in this book, we now critically examine these issues and address how emancipatory research occurs in practice through a critique of domination and surrounding issues of power. Like Danieli and Woodhams (2005), we examine how a broad range of data collection methods and a re-examination of analysis and evaluation can be of greater benefit to disabled communities and create a more critically reflective research. Hence, it is the purpose of what now follows in this book to ascertain how exactly research design and practice can create emancipatory outcomes more skilfully through the emancipatory paradigm and how the nature of emancipation needs a more precise definition.

A rundown of the chapters

To address these issues, we have curated the following chapters to examine the development of emancipatory participatory methodology.

Chapter 2 examines the development of emancipatory participatory methodology and has a more detailed exposition of its roots. It analyzes existing models of researching through emancipatory and participatory research, defines these methodologies, and studies different aspects of this form of research. In this chapter, we also show how the participatory model is a contemporary research methodology designed to include stakeholders, users of technology and visitors to cultural institutions in the development of their own data, ethics, and analysis. This model also allows participants to guide the form of data that are collected, critically evaluate existing methodologies, and provide feedback on inclusion. Finally, this chapter also discusses the application of ethics in emancipatory and participatory studies in relation to existing codes and guidelines.

Chapter 3 is a case study of a small-scale emancipatory investigation that was conducted with the participation of staff members with invisible

Introduction 5

disabilities at the University of Bath. This case study was chosen as it represents a small-scale project researching attitudes to staff members with invisible disabilities at the University of Bath, UK. The project aimed to make recommendations on equality and diversity to the university's management and to reduce future instances of discrimination. It was motivated by a lack of research focusing on disabled academics in the UK and the need to investigate the specific contexts that form disability culture in higher education. Data were collected for this project through broad-ranging interviews, which were designed to gauge the experiences of a small group of disabled academics who had been at the university for differing periods. Following this analysis, recommendations were found to be applicable not only to the University of Bath but also to universities throughout the UK and were written up as such.

Chapter 4 is a case study of a large-scale emancipatory participatory study that was conducted in four cities over three countries. ARCHES began as a European Union Horizon 2020 cultural access project in 2016 to develop accessible technologies as a means of promoting inclusion for disabled people in cultural institutions. Its initial participatory group was formed at the Wallace Collection and Victoria and Albert Museum in London in January 2017. From the outset, it was understood that project participants included all those who visited or communicated with these groups in any regular manner. In this way, a commitment to collective relationships was developed through visits from participating technologists and recordings of activities aimed at addressing problems and questions. The group then produced ways-of-working documents and formed a blueprint for participation, which helped participants recognize that everyone came with skills and experiences, which could lead them in different directions. This model of developing participation was then copied in national museum partners in Madrid and Vienna and a local museum in Oviedo, Spain, from early 2018 through to the summer of 2019.

Chapter 5 concludes with the examination of emancipatory participatory methodology. This chapter concludes the findings of the previous chapters and a discussion on the overlaps between emancipatory and participatory research.

2 Emancipatory and participatory research

Introduction

This chapter discusses the model of the emancipatory paradigm and participatory methodology used in educational studies, which as we stated earlier will be shortened to emancipatory participatory methodology throughout the rest of this book. This methodology was designed to explore the experiences of people with disabilities, while remaining consistent with a theoretical framework of ableism. To do so, this chapter outlines, links, and reviews the consequences of the philosophical orientation and methods of data collection and analysis, which emancipatory participatory studies employ. In addition, it will explore the ethical dimensions of the case studies of emancipatory participatory research in the following two chapters. Before beginning this process, however, it is necessary to define a methodological paradigm in the context of this book and place the approach to research we discuss within this paradigm. For the purposes of this book, methodological paradigms are defined as being what a particular methodology *is*, the ontology of the people who pursue that methodology, and how this methodology differs from others.

According to Markula and Silk (2011), paradigms are approaches to research underpinned by philosophical assumptions, and these assumptions fall into one of the two categories: positivist and postpositivist. These categories are, respectively, associated with the use of primarily quantitative and qualitative methods, and thus the research aims of any given study lead the study toward a positivist or postpositivist paradigm. In addition, it is important to understand how this methodological paradigm affects research involving the study of disability and more importantly people with disabilities. Thus, in the following chapter, we discuss the context and nature of emancipatory and participatory research.

Within the context of education, the emancipatory participatory methodology discussed in this book is both postpositivist and relies heavily on

DOI: 10.4324/9781003083924-2

qualitative data collection methods. These approaches are more appropriate for four reasons: first, they help the research study and capture the deep nuances of experience that is important to help participants "tell their story"; second, the number of potential, let alone actual, participants in an emancipatory and participatory study would often be too low to generate significant and reliable findings for any given research project (Markula and Silk 2011); third, as emancipatory and participatory studies are generally sited within the field of disability studies, these types of study politically and socially reject the assumption that participants with disabilities are homogenous and vulnerable (Nuwagaba and Rule 2015); fourth, postpositivist practices in particular are seen as allied to more ethical forms of research practice and other forms of emancipatory research (Oliver 1992).

Consequently, within this paradigm, postpositivist approaches often employ specific processes in place during the course of their studies to be reflexive and respond to the needs of participants that go beyond regular ethical practices. For example, in emancipatory participatory studies, participants with sensory impairments should receive information and consent forms in more appropriate formats according to their needs and their access preferences—more on this is presented in Chapter 4. Furthermore, participants with intellectual impairments and access needs may require different consent procedures according to their specific needs and preferences. Again, assumptions should also never be made about what these preferences are, as they should be led by the participant (Mietola et al. 2017). Similarly, reflexivity is an important part of research studies influenced by emancipatory principles (Oliver 1992) and should be employed as a tool for making the research process visible or knowable, in whatever form, to all its participants (Markula and Silk 2011). Thus, it is a central tenet of emancipatory participatory studies that all researchers should employ reflexive practice through methods such as research diaries and discussions within groups of participants to continually improve its ethical and practical processes.

Practice as paradigm and methodology

In the field of disability studies, there are two significant definitions of emancipatory research (Barton 2018b). The original definition proposed by writers such as Oliver (1992) and Stone and Priestley (1996) suggests a methodology that claims to offer empowerment through a process based on the principles of the social model. These studies aim to benefit people with disabilities but do not offer opportunities to those beyond this field. By contrast, a later definition that is adopted by Danieli and Woodhams (2005) takes a broader viewpoint of emancipation as a developing model for the broader social good. Subsequently, more contemporary emancipatory participatory studies often move beyond some of the more stringent characteristics of the original model, such as the commitment to the social model of disability, which is now widely criticized, but keep a political commitment to emancipation for people with disabilities. For his part, Barton (2018a) has argued that emancipatory informed research in disability studies is best understood as that which resists inequitable political, cultural, and material circumstances.

Practicing emancipatory research through participatory practice thus rests on two assumptions being made about the nature of emancipatory participatory research: (1) the position of the researcher and the participant and (2) that all research on disability is imbued with some form of values and has the potential to exert power (Oliver 1992). Emancipatory participatory researchers are therefore particularly aware of the potential for themselves to enforce their perspectives on the participants of the research and take steps to avoid this outcome. Instead, these researchers see their role as being to promote the voices and concerns of the participants alone, as objectively and sensitively as possible.

As we stated in the introduction, the approach used during the emancipatory participatory methodology discussed in this book is also largely informed by a contemporary philosophy dating back to the late 1960s and the Independent Living Movement. This movement coined the phrase "Nothing About Us Without Us," which in turn became a rallying cry for people passively institutionalized to take control of their own destiny (Barnes and Mercer 2003). In doing so, this movement asserted:

> [People] with disabilities are human beings with inalienable rights and that these rights can only be secured through collective political action. It arises out of the realization that, as historian Paul Longmore has written, "whatever the social setting and whatever the disability, people with disabilities share a common experience of social oppression."
>
> (Bancroft Library 2004, Para 1)

Subsequently, emancipatory participatory research projects adhere to a further three distinctive principles of independence as an academic researcher:

- The first principle is the researcher's stance on disability research in the social sciences. For instance, the research case study in the following chapter is undertaken by a student on a health and well-being program and aimed to help improve the lives of people with disabilities; this personal aim was supported by the findings of critical investigations of emancipatory disability research in the social sciences; this positionality went beyond defining emancipatory research to make the argument that all disability research in the social sciences has a duty to resist the inequities affecting disabled people and therefore be emancipatory (Barton 2018a).

- The second principle is that the existing literature exploring the institutional culture of disability found in the literature clearly demonstrates that dominant discourses of ability and disability are exclusionary. Thus, such studies automatically discriminate against people with disabilities and access needs.
- The third principle is that emancipatory participatory studies employ postpositivist paradigms, including interpretive, critical, poststructural, and postmodern paradigms. Thus, these studies are primarily differentiated by distinct ontological and epistemological assumptions and the following four research practices (Markula and Silk 2011):

  - A study is designed specifically to address a disabling environment that has been identified by disabled people.
  - Research practice incorporates a plan to create tangible social change by making recommendations designed to improve the disability culture, policies, and practices of the educational institution that is the focus of the study.
  - The researcher has a plan for distribution to the institution being researched, to increase the chance of action being taken, and to promote the voices of the participants.
  - Emancipatory participatory research is concerned with *hearing* and promoting the *voices* of disabled people and includes a participant checking phase to ensure their representation is authentic.

Because of its focus on improving the lives of those that it serves, emancipatory participatory methodology can also include a range of stakeholders, users of technology, and members of institutions in the development of data, as long as its aims are to emancipate. This methodology also allows participants to guide the form of data that are collected, to critically evaluate existing practices, technologies, and policies, and to provide feedback on inclusion and technologies that are created under its auspices.

In practice, emancipatory participatory methodologies are those that promote the engagement of participants to examine their own inclusion and support through self-advocacy and agency (White et al. 2010). Subsequently, forms of participatory practice are implemented in institutional settings by actively involving disabled people in the decision-making and design processes of the research and ethics. In addition, participants are often asked to suggest possible uses and the contexts of uses of the outcomes of the research.

Importantly, the work at hand in emancipatory participatory studies is conducted using a nonclassificatory approach to disability, impairments, and access needs (Rix 2007; Hayhoe 2019). This approach finds that no two people have the same preferences and that people should not be classified according to a single impairment. For instance, participants should not be identified as "sensory impaired" or "learning disabled," and everyone can be assumed to have overlapping impairments of one form or another to some degree or other.

The assumption that all people have access preferences also means that those who run the institutions or those who hold power often also have access preferences themselves. Therefore, the voices of people who are researchers, managers, and educators should be heard in the development of emancipatory participatory studies based on their own personal experience. Furthermore, these voices are seen as being equally valid as those who are recruited because they represented people who it is assumed have difficulties associated with deficit and exclusion by the institution.

What now follows in this chapter is an examination of the ethical issues that often arise during the process of these studies, an examination of sampling and data collection methods that are usually associated with these types of study, the forms of data analysis used in these studies, and the barriers to emancipatory participatory research projects in this order.

Ethical considerations prior to designing emancipatory participatory research

It can be argued that, as the emancipatory paradigm is primarily motivated by an ethic of social justice and participatory methodology is primarily guided by the ethical treatment of its participants, ethics lies at the heart of emancipatory participatory methodology. Consequently, from the start of the research process through to publication, researchers need to adhere closely to and at the same time critically evaluate the relevant ethical guidelines of their discipline or subject area. This can ultimately lead to sensitive and complex dilemmas.

For instance, in the case study in Chapter 3, the research process incorporated the British Sociological Association's (BSA) statement of ethical practice (BSA 2017). An instance of consideration and critical analysis was the BSA's statement:

> Special care should be taken where research participants are particularly vulnerable by virtue of factors such as age, disability, their physical or mental health. Researchers will need to take into account the

legal and ethical complexities involved in those circumstances where there are particular difficulties in eliciting fully informed consent.

(BSA 2017, p. 6)

From this statement, it was understood that the first sentence implied that any participant with a disability could be "particularly vulnerable," a statement that was fundamentally at odds with the purpose of the study. In particular, the perspective of traditional models of disability studies on this issue is that it is disabling and discriminatory to assume that someone with a disability is particularly vulnerable (Oliver 1992). Consequently, for the study to continue forward as a piece of emancipatory participatory research, it had to reject this assumption yet continue to adhere to its other suggested procedures.

However, during the writing of this book, it was also decided that rejecting substantial elements of the BSA's code had the potential to be equally problematic. In particular, as mentioned in the second sentence of the aforementioned statement, there are impairments, special needs, and disabilities that affect the ability of people to give their fully informed consent. Furthermore, the topics of disability and experiences of impairment, special needs, and disability can be sensitive (Durham et al. 2014), thus collecting data using participatory practice without due consideration of that fact could itself breach the BSA (2017) guidelines. Consequently, given these circumstances, it was decided that the most ethical course of action was to

- reject the assumption that disabled research participants were universally vulnerable, while accepting that specific participants may be so;
- exclude potential participants whose impairments could impact their ability to give informed consent, while recognizing that doing so is a limitation of the study that further research could ideally resolve later.

For those studies that require it, during emancipatory participatory studies, the first stage of anonymization should go beyond simply changing the names of participants by removing all irrelevant personal information during transcription. This irrelevant information can include deleting all specific descriptions of their impairment, special need, or disability. Furthermore, when referring to a participant with a specific impairment, no reference to any other details of that person should be included in the transcript or analysis of their data.

Upon recruiting participants to the study, anonymity should also be maintained by asking the participants to contact the researcher individually should they be interested in taking part, thus reducing the risk of allowing participants to be identified by others. The recruitment procedures then target as many members of the institution that is the focus of the study as possible to prevent limiting the participant pool to an even smaller and more identifiable population.

Bias, reflexivity, organizational impact, and research quality

Researcher bias occurs when the perspective of the researcher influences the design, practice, and presentation of a piece of research and is thought of in a number of research traditions as a factor that needs to be eliminated (Markula and Silk 2011). In postpositivist traditions, including poststructuralism, it is accepted that researcher bias cannot be avoided because the researcher is present at all stages of the research process, and even the decision to minimize bias is based on the researcher's perspective. Instead, many postpositivist studies attempt to manage researcher bias by making it visible through practices such as reflexivity (Finlay and Gough 2003).

Reflexive practices during emancipatory participatory studies largely include two elements: the first element is constant attention to the potential ethical consequences of each research design decision and the processes of implementing and presenting the research; the second element is positionality, which is the feminist research practice of being aware of the influence of the researcher's own embodiment (Nencel 2014). Evidence of the attention to the emancipatory consequences of the research design should also be constantly collected and evaluated during emancipatory participatory studies and recorded, often through reflective diaries.

Following this reflection, research practices during the data collection process should be guided by considerations taken from these diaries and the researcher's concern that their embodied experience may potentially elicit a response from the participants (Ostrove and Rinaldi 2013). The researcher should also be aware that the findings can reflect badly on the institution that is the focus of the study, as instances of ableism, prejudice, or discrimination emerge from the data.

Consequently, sensitivity to what are wider social and cultural processes is imperative in emancipatory participatory research. In addition, members of these institutions, both with and without disabilities, should be considered, and importantly emancipatory participatory methodology should not be thought of as a moral crusade. Furthermore, ableism, prejudice, or discrimination should not be assumed, as there is the potential that instances should take place. However, for the researcher to ethically reflect on practice in general, at least some reflexions of these instances in this context were necessary, and sensitivities should ultimately be considered alongside the need to identify social exclusion.

For instance, in the case studies in Chapters 3 and 4, the locations of the research are identified, as they were also identified in previous publications

Emancipatory and participatory research 13

and were highly identifiable. Furthermore, in the case study presented in Chapter 3, which was focused on the University of Bath, the institution was the place where the researcher studied and that held the dissertation's copyright. In addition, museums that were the focus of the research in Chapter 4 were often the employers of many of the education officers administering the participatory groups.

In such circumstances, a higher ethical imperative should be considered. That is to say, the institution that is the focus of research, where the researcher is studying in or is employed by, should in no way overshadow the reporting of exclusion in the institution. In addition, should the researcher not act on his or her findings when such experiences are uncovered, the project will have failed as an emancipatory participatory study and a project identifying itself with disability studies.

In terms of the quality of the data that are collected during an emancipatory participatory study, there are no universally accepted judgment criteria that measure the ethical quality of such qualitative research. This lack of universal agreement on quality is largely due to the diverse research philosophies, practices, and forms of representation found in postpositivist paradigms (Markula and Silk 2011). To make this situation more complex, disability studies can be said to generally lack any criteria for judging quality beyond a commitment to the political goals of the field; this is an ideal that is codified in two sets of standards for emancipatory research (Barnes and Mercer 2010).

Oliver (1992) argues that the ethics of an emancipatory paradigm should be judged by its adherence to *emancipatory methods* alone. However, Danieli and Woodhams (2005) take an opposing view, arguing instead that emancipatory research cannot be assessed until after the fact. That is to say, emancipatory studies are based on the consequences and changes that happen after the study has finished.

However, as the latter criteria are often difficult to ascertain, particularly as the changes recommended by many studies occur only years after research has been published, the former criteria are often regarded as being more practical. This criterion can usually be achieved by taking into consideration the voices and concerns of participants with disabilities as well as aiming for an emancipatory outcome throughout the research process.

Intervention development and participant and participant observer satisfaction

An outcome of the adoption of emancipatory participatory methodology that includes participants with disabilities is that ethical interventions need to be developed in response to the self-identified needs of the participants

(Oliver 1992). In many circumstances, frameworks such as Barnes and Mercer's (2010) review of the societal barriers faced by people with disabilities can be used as a template for the types of intervention that will take place. These include barriers to accessing physical spaces, information, and psychological support, and these examples can lead to the respective interventions such as improving transport provision or enforcing regulations on reasonable access modifications; multiplatform information access; and creating peer counseling services for people receiving institutional support.

Feedback on the study and the applied interventions from the participants must also be collected for the study to adhere to its emancipatory paradigm of accountability to people with disabilities (Oliver 1992). This form of feedback can be gathered from both the individual participants and the institutions that are the focus of study to gain a diverse range of perspectives on study outcome and processes, respectively. This feedback can be gathered via a range of qualitative data collection methods, needs to be conducted at different stages of the study, and then analyzed thematically.

A measure of the interventions and by extension participants' quality of life, including the changes in participants' quality of life as a result of a study, is essential for the study to prove it has had a positive impact on the lives of the participants. The data collection and subsequent analysis of these changes in quality of life will typically take place through a transdisciplinary framework adapted from quality-of-life measures from psychology, health economics, and occupational therapy. These will be developed with an awareness of the principles of emancipatory research.

In addition, economic measures of the quality-of-life improvements are often used to measure the effects of elements such as the impact on career and life-style measurements. This also has the potential to identify a preliminary measurement of the feasibility of similar interventions being employed as a routine part of welfare policies in research projects and thus can become the focus of emancipatory participatory research.

Intervention guidelines such as those laid down in interdisciplinary and transdisciplinary enquiry, such as those discussed in Chapter 4, find that researchers and collaborators given equal status and opportunity to contribute feel more represented during group practice. In this particular study, these guidelines were encoded as *ways of working* developed by the participatory groups after debate and the sharing of previous experiences of the research (Hayhoe 2020).

In small-scale studies with a single researcher, intervention guidelines should be considered by the researcher in partnership with the participants. In large-scale studies, where a number of researchers work together to develop a unified approach, the team as a whole should negotiate these guidelines to facilitate an equal and democratic approach. Simultaneously, participant representatives in these studies should also be trained to provide oversight to maximize flexibility and equitability of the coherence of this process.

Designing an emancipatory participatory study

Recruitment procedures, informed consent, and participant information

Given its self-selecting nature, the process of sampling used in emancipatory participatory methodology is often purposive sampling (Patton 2002), as cases that are information rich and relevant to the study can target criteria used for inclusion. For instance, a number of emancipatory participatory studies use the initial stages of constructing a sample to recruit trusted "middle people."

The middle people chosen for the research can, once the study has been designed and ethical clearance received, forward an official recruitment email to groups, such as departmental staff or students, that have potential participants. However, it is imperative that such middle people, as they themselves have no ethical clearance, are not the contact point for any replies to these emails. Subsequently, any messages researchers send should contain a request that recipients who are interested in taking part should reply directly to a named researcher who has ethical clearance. An example draft of an email to middle people and an official recruitment email can be found in the Appendix.

Informed consent is the right of all potential research participants to be informed about the research and their rights as participants prior to taking part. To have to give that consent formally before data collection can begin is not only an essential part of any emancipatory participatory research project but also one of the cornerstones of social methods (BSA 2017). Consequently, almost all university-based ethical committees will insist on informed consent and the nondeception of research participants no matter what methodology is used, with few exceptions such as double-blind, randomized control trials. For instance, the case study in Chapter 3 followed the guidelines and had to meet the approval of the University of Bath Research Ethics Approval Committee for Health's (REACH). These guidelines provided a strict procedure for ensuring research participants were informed and consented via an information memo outlining the project, which needed to be signed by the participants to acknowledge their consent.

To maximize the anonymity of participants for studies that require it, only a brief description of the group of participants needs to be given when information about participants is being recorded. This point is particularly important for participants whose impairments or disabilities are invisible and are only referred to in greater detail within the findings, where their specific role or personal history is relevant to other participants' experiences. For instance, studies may have participants with varying levels of career, membership, or studentship within a given institution, from those who step into an institution on the day of the study to those whose whole career has been spent in the institution. These influences, and others such as sexuality, class, and race, should not be directly addressed during the data collection, as the focus should continue to be the experiences of disability and because the details that would need to be given to explore their intersectionality may compromise anonymity, but as some briefly appeared as relevant to the participants, they could be the focus of future research.

The raw data for emancipatory participatory studies are almost entirely qualitative in nature and collected over the course of all the participant sessions planned during the research, allowing data and the participants' opinions to develop and mature. This data collection can be in any form, if it is accessible to the participants themselves, it is agreed upon by all the participants and it provides viable feedback to participants. In the studies the authors have been involved in, data collection methods have included everything from participant observations, where participants and researchers are all invited to record their observations, to participant diaries, unstructured and semi-structured interviews, art-making exercises, and focus groups.

Whatever methods are used, however, data collection sessions need to focus on the issues that are of interest to disability studies, such as the areas in which participants might have had experiences of the effects of their impairment, access issues, or special needs; notions of ability and disability and its role in the institution that is at the heart of the research; participants' thoughts and feelings about those experiences; and how the institution responds to impairment, access needs, special needs, and disability. This data collection itself should also be participant led, with the researcher following up on points that, when it has been agreed, are particularly relevant to the research and that seem to be of important to the participants.

Participant inclusion and exclusion criteria

The aim of emancipatory participatory studies is to recruit an appropriate number of participants suitable for the nature of the study as in-depth qualitative research focusing on individual experiences (Markula and Silk 2011). As can be seen in the two case studies presented in the following two chapters, this number can range from hundreds to five participants, although any fewer may diminish the depth of the participatory process. There is a precedent of similarly sized projects in disability studies (Barnes 2003) and

Emancipatory and participatory research 17

in the five participants used in another piece of poststructural research of the experiences of disabled academics specifically (Waterfield et al. 2018).

The initial criteria for inclusion in the participatory groups in this form of research include (1) participants should self-identify as disabled, special needs, or access needs that necessitate support through the institution that is the focus of the research, such as a school or university; (2) or/and the participants must support people with disabilities or access needs, or be working to develop policies, learning strategies, or technologies that support people with disabilities. These criteria ensure that the participants' experiences are relevant to the study at the location of the research and that their experiences are those that reflect the current and recent period of time. These factors are important given Foucault's (1983) conception of discourses as being spatially and temporally specific.

There are three reasons for using self-identification:

1 *The confidentiality of participants, and the identification of their disability, is paramount if participants choose to stay anonymous.* If the participants of a given study are limited to those officially registered by an institution, and a list of all participants who self-identify as disabled is made public, then this action could potentially risk publicly identifying people who may not want their disability to be made public. Thus, letting participants know about the ramifications of the study and its dissemination is vital.

2 *Using diverse, subjective criteria for deciding disability can be problematic, exclude participants, and remove agency from disabled people* (Miskovic and Gabel 2012). Using any form of subjective definition of disability, either medical or those characteristics that are particular to any form of impairment, such as sensory impairment, blindness, or deafness, runs contrary to the ethos of a Foucauldian approach. This approach attempts to remain critically aware of the nature and consequences of such biopolitical discourses (Tremain 2015).

3 *Previous research on disability revealed that disclosure is an issue for some disabled people* (see, e.g., Ewens et al. 2011); *consequently research that assumes disclosure takes place does not reflect disability experiences and limits the participant pool.* This is an important criterion but one that needs to be handled carefully during any given study as it is difficult to implement. For example, during studies, it may be found that disclosure of disability can be amended in practice if participants state that they have an impairment but don't necessarily consider themselves to be disabled or have a disability. The response and implications of this situation are referred to in the following case studies in this book and show that this criterion must remain flexible.

18 *Emancipatory and participatory research*

By contrast, the only criterion for exclusion advocated in emancipatory participatory studies is that participants must have the ability to give informed consent or informed assent, to safeguard the participant from manipulation by researchers and fellow participants (BSA 2017). The absence of voices of people with such impairments should be considered a potential weakness of the emancipatory participatory methodology for two reasons. First, the effects of learning access issues and discursive construction of severe learning impairments heavily interact with the demands and discursive construction of the exclusion of people with disabilities (Waterfield et al. 2018). Second, this exclusion contradicts the element of the inclusion criteria that participants should not be excluded because of subjective criteria, as being unable to consent or assent denotes an impairment to learning and communication. However, given the higher ethical order of assent and consent in the emancipatory paradigm and participatory research, this is a necessary exception.

From transcription to critical thematic or theory-based analysis

During emancipatory participatory studies, accessible transcription is a significant precursor to developing the analysis of qualitative data. Transcription can be understood as a form of translation and, as such, has the potential for misinterpretation on the part of the transcriber (Gillham 2005). To minimize the potential for such misinterpretation, and to capture as many of the subtle details of the participants' voices as possible, it is considered that the ideal is to transcribe the interviews verbatim. However, the reality of small-scale studies, particularly those for postgraduate or doctoral dissertations, is that delays and lack of funding may leave insufficient time to transcribe entire interviews or to make them fully accessible in all formats, such as Braille or signed.

In small-scale studies, it may be decided to develop accessible notes outlining the points recorded during data collection and to only transcribe sections that are significant to the participants, such as tensions arising from the research or jarring experiences. After the initial analysis had taken place, this process can be repeated through further data collection and key quotes that align with the initial analysis noted as aligning with the themes that continue to emerge. Although this method is undoubtedly less thorough than verbatim transcription, it has been argued that the merger of transcription and analysis cannot necessarily be separated from the interpretation of socially constructed data (Fairclough 2001).

Following transcription, critical forms of thematic or case study analysis can be thought of as the hallmark of an emancipatory participatory study, as such critical analysis reveals the structures of power that govern the experiences of the participants (Cohen et al. 2005). This focus on the nature of power particularly aligns with the Foucauldian theoretical framework at the heart of an emancipatory paradigm (Markula and Silk 2011). In addition, representational concerns need to be considered during when choosing thematic analysis or case study. In this respect, theory-based analysis should also be used to promote a stronger link to the academic literature in the specific field being investigated and is required to explore the philosophical assumptions of the constructions of disability in significant depth.

Another hallmark of emancipatory participatory research design is participant checking procedures, which are designed to ensure that participants are satisfied with how data are collected and interpreted and endorse that their voices are being represented. A common participant checking procedure is to discuss the themes that emerge through analysis and which the researcher feels represent an aggregate of experiences with the participants at regular intervals and to present any quotes that are to be used for dissemination. Importantly, engaging participants throughout the analysis and encouraging them to contribute to the evaluation and presentation of their data provide agency as well as ensuring the authenticity of the representation (Smith-Chandler and Swart 2014).

In the following chapters, this methodology of sampling, data collection, and then analysis is shown in practice through the development of two case studies of emancipatory participatory studies. The first case study is a small-scale project conducted for a master's dissertation, whereas the second case study is a large multi-country study of museum access. What is evident in both is that participatory research in both large- and small-scale studies is a process of compromise and managing tensions. However, it is in the process of compromise and the management of tensions that the richest understanding of the social and cultural nature of disability and participatory studies can be observed.

3 Case study of a small-scale university-based postgraduate project

Introduction

This chapter presents a case of an emancipatory influenced project that was informed by participatory methodology for a postgraduate degree in the social sciences and examining higher education. It describes how emancipatory data collection, analysis, and representation procedures were developed and implemented as part of a small-scale research project, and then developed for publication and assessment as a successful Master of Research (MRes) dissertation. Although its strategies and techniques are unique and adapted from standard research degree practices, they are also applicable to other postgraduate degrees or final-year undergraduate dissertations.

This original research project was titled "An emancipatory investigation of the experiences of academics with invisible disabilities at the University of Bath." It was designed to hear, engage with, and promote the voices of disabled academics working at the University of Bath, UK, as well as to provide guidance on how to address the inequalities that the project brought to light. The aim of what now follows in this chapter is to present a realistic application of emancipatory and participatory considerations in the postgraduate research process; to show how such considerations can shape projects; and to highlight the implications of these studies on practice and how these studies can be designed and presented as part of a postgraduate research assignment.

The study was unique in its application of an emancipatory paradigm as it was a project working with disabled academics at a single university by a master's student, who was developing his own skills and knowledge of the field himself. Thus, one of the prominent issues of the study was power and the awkward nature of researching with participants who potentially have more power than the student who is undertaking a study as part of their assessment. The approach used to develop the project was applied in three sections: First, a critical literature review located the project within the

DOI: 10.4324/9781003083924-3

field of disability studies, outlined the context of disability in academia, and enabled an appropriate research question to be identified; second, primary data were collected using semi-structured interviews with academics who self-identified as having a disability; third, the interview data were analyzed using *critical thematic analysis*, which also engaged the participants in checking procedures that they had contributed to themselves. In this chapter, the second and third stages of this process are presented as a single case study to provide a model of the preparation and application of fieldwork.

The context of disability in the university and what follows in this chapter

The research project was initially planned because rhetorical evidence was uncovered at a local level to show that academics with disabilities were being put at a severe disadvantage compared to able-bodied academics. In addition, it was observed that the experience of academics with disabilities is an underresearched topic in the literature, and it was felt that there was a potentially widespread exclusion in universities that was poorly understood and infrequently recognized. This issue of exclusion was not a local issue, however, and a small number of previous studies identified causes of disadvantage, including the construction of disability and neoliberal performance standards (Waterfield et al. 2018); the interaction of impairment effects within higher education environments (Williams and Marvin 2015); and a lack of sufficient support systems or a culture that is welcoming to disability (Ewens et al. 2011).

The ontological approach this study took was the Foucauldian theoretical approach discussed in the previous chapter, which necessarily led to the emancipatory participatory practice that is the focus of this book. Furthermore, to embed the principle of impact into the theoretical approach, the concept of ableism was used. Ableism is a theoretical lens that suggests that *able-bodiedness* is assumed and discriminates in its use as a principle in the organization of society (Campbell 2009). The advantage of focusing on ableism is that it shares a Foucauldian approach to understanding power, but in a manner that enables impact to be made, as if findings show ableism, it follows that their cause is discriminatory, and the emancipatory principles of social change should necessarily apply. Subsequently, the overarching research question that the study attempted to answer was as follows:

Do the experiences of academics with disabilities who are currently employed by the University of Bath uncover examples of ableism and exclusion?

22 A small university-based postgraduate project

The description of this project is now split into the following three sections: Methodology and methods, with this section including a discussion on the overall methodologies, data collection, and restrictions encountered; the findings of the semi-structured interviews, with this section including a summary of findings presented by theme; and a discussion of the findings, with this section examining the findings in relation to the research question and existing theory and exploring potential implications.

Summary of the methodologies and methods

Research methodologies

The research design principles were underpinned by a contemporary understanding of the emancipatory research paradigm, which forms a large part of this book. In practice, these principles influenced the design of the project through three modes of emancipatory participatory methodology.

The first mode of methodology was the subject of the research, as to resist inequitable settings, the research needed to focus on specific episodes that could be inequitable. The choice to focus on disabled academics began as one of the author's own personal interest, as he studied initially material focusing on disabled students prior to the project but noticed that studies mentioning disabled academics were rare. However, this interest and the suspicion that disabled academics may face inequitable circumstances were not sufficient justification on its own. I needed to be able to show a gap in the research and, in the case of emancipatory research, the nature of the potentially inequitable circumstances. After an initial, informal scoping review of the literature showed the importance of these issues, the critical literature review was used to formally claim that the environment of academia is hostile to disabled academics.

The second mode was the considerations of the potential consequences of all the research decisions about the participants and the research aims that were made throughout the research process. This was necessary because of the acknowledgment that emancipatory researchers must make of the power embedded in the research process, originating in the philosophical assumptions that the study makes about the nature of research, the relative positions of the researcher and participant, and the social and cultural *nature* of disability. These considerations are shown throughout this summary of methodologies and methods.

The third mode that was considered was the emancipatory principles that affected the research design through its impact, objectives, and aims, which in turn led to the development with the participants of a set of targets to achieve through the research. For instance, if the research did not attempt to improve the circumstances of the participants and disabled academics in general, then it was felt that it would fail in its aim to be an emancipatory project.

Data collection methods

During this project, primary data were collected through semi-structured interviews and included a participant checking phase. The aim of this part of the data collection process was to recruit four to seven participants, a suitable number for in-depth qualitative research focusing on participant experiences (Markula and Silk 2011). During this phase of the data collection, the initial inclusion criteria for participation was that the participants must be currently employed by the University of Bath in an academic or researcher position and self-identify as disabled. These criteria ensured that the participants' involvement would be relevant to the study and reflected their then present and recent experiences.

The decision to get participants to self-identify as disabled was made for three reasons: (1) if the participants had been limited to those officially *registered* as disabled by the university and that list of registered staff members was to be made public, then it would increase the chances of the participants being identified; (2) using the university's criteria for registering disability can exclude participants and remove agency from those staff members with what they felt were disabilities, but remained unrecognized as such (Miskovic and Gabel 2012); (3) previous research on disability at the university revealed that disclosure was an issue for some disabled students and staff (Ewens et al. 2011); thus, it was felt that if the study only used participants who felt comfortable disclosing their disability, it would be less able to reflect the spectrum of disabled experiences and would reduce the pool of participants. This criterion was amended in practice after several potential participants stated that they have an impairment but did not necessarily consider themselves to be disabled, and this amendment was reflected in the findings and discussion of the project.

Subsequently, the only exclusion criterion used during the study was that the participants should not have an impairment that could affect their ability to give informed consent, such as staff members with extreme communication and learning disabilities (BSA 2017). The absence of the voices of people with communication and learning disabilities was a potential weakness of the study design, especially as the effects and use of language surrounding severe learning disabilities interact with the demands and popular understanding of academic employment (Waterfield et al. 2018). However, in the end, it had no bearing on the research as none of the potential participants had such powerful learning or communication disabilities.

To gain their informed consent, the participants were given an information sheet outlining the project and their consent was recorded with a signature, a procedure followed the guidelines given by the faculty research committee at the university. The project design led to a targeted pool of potential participants, who self-identified as having a disability. To make as many members of this group as possible aware about the study and the participant inclusion criteria, intermediaries were recruited, and these intermediaries sent out emails to groups of academics as well as by word of mouth. In this way, all direct communication between the potential participants and the researcher was at the behest of the participants. The maximized recruitment pool and participant-initiated recruitment process minimized the identification of the participants.

The research included both adult male and female participants, their impairments were all invisible, and in the final analysis, they were only referred to more specifically where their specific nature was relevant to their experiences. The participants had varying lengths of academic career, from being near to the beginning of their careers to having over 15 years of experience in postdoctoral work. These variables and others such as their sexuality, class, and ethnicity were not directly addressed by the interview guide, as it was the intention of the research to focus on impairment and disability alone. This decision was taken because the details that would need to be given to explore the participants' intersectionality may have compromised their anonymity in such a local study, although these variables also appeared to be relevant to some participants' experiences and thus it was decided that this could be the focus of future research with a differently secure process. This process was supported by the thematic representation of the data and impairment not being discussed in conjunction with potentially identifying information.

The raw data were collected over the course of a single semi-structured interview with each of the participants leading their discussions. Each of the participant interviews that lasted between 25 minutes and 1 hour was recorded as a secured voice file on a laptop, and each of the interviews took place on the university campus in a secured room where the participant felt comfortable. The interview plan was designed to outline the areas that participants might have had experienced the effects of their disability in their role at the university, their thoughts and feelings about those experiences, and how the university responded to their impairments and disabilities. As stated earlier, the interviews were primarily participant led, with the researcher following up on points that were particularly relevant to the research or seemed to be of import to the participants but using predeveloped lines of open questions if the discussion moved to far away from the research topic. The scope of the plan and the role of the interviewer were designed in accordance with Markula and Silk's (2011) recommendation that there should be an awareness of the importance of the role of the participant in emancipatory research.

Methods of data analysis and representation

When planning the transcription of the interviews, there was an awareness of the power imbued in the research process and the dangers that misstranscribing the data might misrepresent what the participants meant. To minimize the potential for such misinterpretation, and to capture as many of the nuances of the participants' experiences as possible, it was hoped to transcribe the interviews verbatim prior to analysis. However, the delays imposed upon the start of the project by the faculty's research committee and the MRes deadline mandated by the program timetable left insufficient time to conduct this process. Instead, a compromise was made and briefer notes outlining the interviews with largely transcribed sections, which the researcher and participants felt were most important, were created. After an initial analysis had taken place, this process was repeated, and additional notes of key quotes were made to align with the themes that appeared to emerge. Although this method was undoubtedly less thorough than verbatim transcription, the merger of the transcription and analysis is supported by authors who have noted that transcription cannot necessarily be separated from interpretation (Fairclough 2001).

When deciding which form of analysis might be appropriate for this project, the emancipatory methodology of the study and its concern with the structures of power in educational institutions were tied together. Critical analyses were found to be an effective tool in this respect, as it identified these power structures and linked them to the participants' most potent experiences (Cohen et al. 2005). This aim is also noted as being appropriate for emancipatory and Foucauldian approaches alike (Danieli and Woodhams 2005; Markula and Silk 2011). In addition, during this phase of the analysis, what was termed *participant checking procedures* were developed to ensure that the participants were satisfied with how their interviews were interpreted and their *voices* were represented.

The procedure for this *checking* instrument was to email the participants the themes that the researcher felt represented their experiences and any quotes that were to be used in the eventual report of the project, with their changes being integrated into a further stage of analysis. This participant checking procedure subsequently contributed significantly to the analysis and presentation of the data and provided a high degree of agency to the participants as well as ensuring the authenticity of their representation in the project (Smith-Chandler and Swart 2014), a strategy that fulfilled a requirement of the emancipatory paradigm of the research (Danieli and Woodhams 2005).

For practical reasons, however, slight changes to this *participant checking procedure* needed to be made reflexively as the analysis progressed. For instance, the original plan was to participant check after initial data analysis had taken place and before a formal write up began. At this stage, though, it was felt that the theory-based analysis was not thorough enough, and so it was decided to implement an iterative data analysis process to be conducted alongside writing the discussion chapter. This meant that the participant checking was delayed by approximately three weeks but resulted in a more coherent line of critical analysis and reduced the need to repeatedly contact the participants as the analysis and focus of the discussions shifted and unfolded.

The findings of the *critical thematic analysis* were thus presented in the final dissertation as themes supported by direct quotes. This form of presentation reduced the chance that the participants may be identified by removing the ability to link multiple pieces of data as a pattern and so build a more detailed and coherent picture of individual participants. The representation of the theory-based analysis is found primarily in the discussion and does not include any new data. Throughout the research process, the British Sociological Association's statement of ethical practice was used to inform the design and development of the data collection (BSA 2017),

> Special care should be taken where research participants are particularly vulnerable by virtue of factors such as age, disability, their physical or mental health. Researchers will need to take into account the legal and ethical complexities involved in those circumstances where there are particular difficulties in eliciting fully informed consent.
> (BSA 2017, p. 6.)

From this quote, however, the first sentence was interpreted to imply that any participant with a disability should be considered "particularly vulnerable," a statement that was fundamentally disagreed with in this project and against the paradigm of emancipation. That is to say, just because a person has a disability, it should not be automatically assumed that they were not capable of standing up for themselves or advocating for themselves. Thus, this assumption was felt to be symbolic and representative of historically patronizing attitudes, and it is disabling and discriminatory to assume that someone with a disability is more vulnerable than any other (Oliver 1992).

After rejecting components of the BSA code and recognizing that it had the potential to be problematic, it was equally recognized that the topic of disability and the experiences of impairment and disability can be sensitive

(Durham et al. 2014). Consequently, interviewing without due consideration of these sensitivities could have unnecessarily and unfairly breached the code without due consideration (BSA 2017). Thus, the decision was taken to adapt the following ethical practices and ontological positions from the code:

1   Although the assumption that disabled research participants are not universally vulnerable, some specific participants were thought to be so, as members of every social group are to a greater or lesser extent.
2   It was decided to exclude potential participants whose impairments could impact their ability to give informed consent, while recognizing that doing so was a limitation of the study, and thus, follow-up research could ideally resolve in future years.
3   It was decided to approach the interviews with an awareness that the topics discussed may be distressing and to pre-emptively act to minimize this risk by making sure the participants were aware that the interview may have touched on sensitive subjects, that they thus had the right to withdraw at any time, and that they could get contact details for organizations that provided support should they need them.

In addition to the external ethical issues addressed throughout the study, during the research design process, the emancipatory nature of the study meant that the researcher had to be aware of his own impact on the participants. Reflective practice, a postpositivist technique of managing researcher bias (Finlay and Gough 2003), was adopted as an accepted practice within disability studies to address these issues of bias (Barnes and Mercer 2010). The practices that were subsequently applied were constant attention to the potential emancipatory consequences of each research design and implementation, and positionality. Positionality, or awareness of the influence of the researcher's own embodied nature and physical presence (Nencel 2014), was particularly important because interviewers' dis/abled bodies can affect participants' responses negatively and unfairly (Ostrove and Rinaldi 2013).

One way in which it was felt that the researcher affected the study was his position as a student researcher, which made his own institution both identifiable and the focus of potentially critical attention. However, should there have been any instances of prejudice or discrimination, the university would have been able to address them through its disciplinary process, follow their inclusion and antidiscrimination policies, and defend the position of its own disabled academics. Therefore, from the researcher's own perspective, the potential benefits of the research were felt to outweigh the potential harm to the public image of the university the project could cause, and the issue was thus not raised as an area of concern by the faculty's board of ethics.

Findings that arose from the study

Identity and impairments

The findings themselves were interesting in building an understanding of the emancipatory participatory process, particularly the construction of the participant's disabled social and cultural identity. For instance, participants almost exclusively described their own disability as being based on a combination of medical diagnoses and their individualized experiences of impairment, as opposed to the project's theoretically based definition of disability as societally imposed disadvantage.

Only one participant linked their disability to a political status or act, initially saying that they "have difficulty calling what I have a disability" as the nature of their condition was almost entirely negated by medical support. This support could be compared to a friend of theirs, who had a severe hearing impairment, and thus, "I would have felt like it was cheating. To put myself on the same level." However, after an encounter with a disability activist, the participant changed their mind and spoke about the importance of raising awareness of disability issues and disabled people by calling it what it is. Two more participants echoed this sentiment and described their struggle to exactly call their chronic pain a disability, because of their variable nature, "it's not a matter of ability- can I do it yes I can, but I'm in pain [when I do it]."

This being said, when this issue was explored further, it was observed that the medical diagnoses made a difference. In particular, one participant was challenged on a personal level as the diagnosis shifted to how he saw himself, to acknowledge that he could be considered to be disabled and that, for his health, there would be things that he couldn't do. On the other hand, having a diagnosis and being able to call it a disability empowered the second participant, thus legitimizing their experiences to themselves, and for colleagues where it could provide "proof" of the invisible "I knew it, I'm not crazy. I'm not making up this pain, it's there."

Three of the participants also struggled communicating the impact of their invisible condition without revealing diagnoses, with one participant being concerned that "it will be perceived as a weakness, perceived as an excuse. And particularly because if any of my colleagues, my seniors, look at me, they can't see any explanation." Furthermore, only one of the participants viewed being disabled as central to their identity or wanted it to define their relationships. For another participant, however, being a person with a disability became a part of their life's narrative, both as a hardship and as something with disadvantages, although they felt that hard work, determination, and luck have made them what they are today.

Meaningfully, the three participants who did not completely see themselves as disabled would not have become participants had the researcher been strict with the initial inclusion criterion, "self-identification as disabled." They responded similarly to the recruitment email, saying that they would like to be involved but they were unsure if they qualified for the inclusion criteria, stated their diagnosis, and asked the primary researcher if they were suitable. This response was not anticipated by the researcher, where only self-identifying as disabled but not being registered as such within their place of work was anticipated. The decision to relax the inclusion criteria was made because, following a conversation over email, the participants were revealed to be either registered with the university as disabled or to have the social effects their impairment were relevant to their academic experiences.

The impact of impairment on the participants' work lives and careers was significant for almost all the participants. They were seen as a cause of worry and stress, had caused significant periods of less productive work if not complete absences, affected career decisions, and hindered the career progression of participants. In particular, the facets of the participants' working lives that were impacted often included teaching, as experiencing a flare-up of a condition could stop the performance aspect of lecturing, researching, if impairment effects limited the amount or precision of reading or writing, and indeed being able to work at all, if it became a struggle to get out of bed. In terms of the consequences of these experiences, when asked if their condition had been a barrier, one participant responded:

> Huge. It's also a facilitator. I'm in the job that it's hardest for me to do because it's all about writing and presenting and arguing and it's all high pressured and hugely precise. So you're not just writing stuff, you're writing stuff for an international audience where you're meant to be at the top level, and writing's really hard for me. So it is, but I also come at things differently often from how other people in the room come in things. . . . So yes it has been a barrier. I suffer hugely from stress and that's linked to having this condition and being under high pressure to do this kind of work.

In addition, one participant felt that her career had been limited because of the extra time and effort she had to dedicate to fulfilling certain tasks as part of their role took time away from conducting research, while another participant was worried that in the future she would have to ask themselves "will I be able to do that?" too see if her condition would permit her to take the jobs she would like to do. Another point that was repeatedly emphasized during the interviews was the consequences of the experiences of impairment were not a choice but a physical or psychological manifestation, "sometimes I have to stop because I'm hurting, even when my mind doesn't want to."

Disclosure and academic culture

All the participants disclosed their disability to the university either formally or informally, although for one this was limited to ticking the box, "Yes, I have a disability" on their application form when they applied for their jobs. For the remaining four participants, two disclosed their disability in the period following their diagnosis and two at a significantly later date. The only reason given for any disclosure was to receive accommodation from the university. These accommodations included a range of issues, from requiring a brief absence to get external support to providing support on behalf of academics who were unable to work. Three of the participants were reluctant to disclose issues to the university, with their top concerns being that if they did so they would be seen as different from their colleagues; a fear that if they disclosed their disability, they would face prejudice from other members of the university; and the fear that if they admitted there was something *wrong* with them and their level of *function*, their life at the university would become difficult. For instance, the following are examples of answers given during the interviews highlighting these issues:

> I never tell an employer before I'm employed that I have a disability. It's because I don't think . . . I've been at university in various different places in academia where disability has been talked about very negatively, so I don't . . . I don't out myself until my legs are under the table and I'm in a secure position just in case of prejudice.
>
> I was concerned who would be aware of it and what the label would be.

However, when talking about potential disclosure to students, the consensus was a more open approach that could be beneficial:

> The ability to say that "I understand, I also have a disability and I'm working through it," you can quite physically see the relief that someone says its normal, that they can get the support they need for them.
>
> I tell all of my students about it quite early on, because I think it's important for them to be aware . . . one, if they're disabled that there is someone there who has achieved, but also that is going to be empathetic,

but also for people who aren't to see someone who is disabled to stand in front of them and doing a lecture and performing well.

Despite their concerns over disclosure, none of the participants mentioned facing any prejudice or discrimination from other members of staff while working at the university, with one participant explicitly saying that "I never sensed from my department that it was a factor in how they view me as an employee." Another participant made another possibly more positive comparison, "what was important that was showing your disability . . . acknowledging that there is something that I can't do, is ok here. In [country in mainland Europe, where I'm from] it is different."

The flexibility and, in positions of seniority, security of academic work for academics with a disability was seen as an attractive quality by three of the participants involved in the study. The consequences of impairment that affected four of the participants with little to no notice were somewhat mitigated by their pursuit of research although not the lecturing component of their work. As one participant said, "taking short windows off [work] is not a problem, so to speak, with the nature of the job."

However, overall academic culture was viewed as much more of an issue than it was an advantage, particularly with regards to the amount of work that academics are expected to do, the pressure they can feel themselves under, and how those factors interact with their impairments. In particular, four participants said that anything that makes an academic less productive can damage their career, that the effects of their impairments made them less "quantitatively" productive, and that the effects of their impairments had not been minimized or compensated for. Furthermore, another participant also mentioned how important disabled student support was for that very reason.

The expectation that academics should be "working every hour and doing . . . things in their spare time," coupled with the feeling that there was a need for academics to "work ourselves into the ground," was a sentiment that was highlighted by three participants. However, this sentiment was not one that just affects disabled people, but it was a belief system that was a part of the institutional culture of "the university" and that was, one participant felt, "a problem for all of us [not just disabled academics]." However, this being said the academic working culture particularly affected the participants because of their disabilities, "I can't do that, I can't work every hour . . . it's not a choice that I'm not working every hour."

People who had children, and in particular women who took time off to have children, were also mentioned as being particularly affected by the effects of their disability, largely because the gaps in their research output reflected time off enforced for medical reasons. Thus, the inability to meet a demand to publish constantly, especially when it is used as a deciding factor between candidates for lectureships or more senior posts, was seen as a negative effect of their disability. Furthermore, the drive to achieve these standards has led to one participant hearing of:

> lots of people who are disabled consciously [choosing] not to have children in order to keep up their work ethic, particularly women. And that was something that women academics did previously, but I know disabled women academics who are making those kinds of choices.

Furthermore, a culture of individual competence emerged throughout the interviews, with one participant saying, "There's a department culture, an academic culture, a societal culture about not asking for help, [about] being able to cope." This experience stood in opposition to how disabled people were required to ask for help following a review of academic workload that was not compatible with what was regarded as their lower levels of quantitative productivity. The reaction of three of the participants to this dilemma was to implement private personal coping strategies to be seen as competent, even if, as in the case of all the participants that were interviewed, it was a source of mental pressure and even, in one participant's case, it was to the detriment of their personal health. While these strategies mitigated some of the effects of their impairments, the participants still felt that they were not necessarily enough to negate the effects of their disabilities completely. As one participant said:

> I am fortunate in that I had already established myself, that I had some reputation and therefore it would be much harder to face that, if you were trying to face the condition as a younger person, trying to build a career.

"Elitist" higher educational culture, both in academia as a whole and at the university, was described as "closed," meaning that the visible numbers of disabled academics and disabled students were so low that it was "worrying." As one participant stated, "I don't think there's a culture of talking openly about these kinds of conditions, which resonates with my own concerns." By being examples of successful disabled people, a number of participants also felt that they somehow defied the higher educational culture in which disability was more likely to be seen as a deficit rather than as diversity. This was reinforced by one participant's recollection that they had heard of another academic "being very negative about dyslexic students" and thinking that "they don't believe that a dyslexic person can do such-and-such a job."

The lack of diversity at the university was said to reach further than a "diversity of ability," with ethnic minority, working, and lower middle class, and northern English students also being underrepresented in the institution. These findings became a real issue that required action when the attitude of the university was experienced by a participant as being discriminatory and divisive. As she stated, "I sometimes get the sense that our university does widening participation type activities for the image. They do it, but maybe they do it to look good rather than truly believing." This absence of willingness to *actually* level entry for higher education is also evident in how workplace assessments were experienced by another participant:

> A couple of times those conversations have felt like they're checking that I don't want to complain about anything rather than ensuring that there is anything else. "Check you don't need this, check you don't want this." I felt that they were kind of writing stuff down saying that I didn't want the support in case I later said I wasn't supported they could say "well you said you didn't need this." So, it feels like the university is as much evidencing that it is doing the right thing as it is actually being supportive.

Support

Through participants' experience of workplace culture and access to and provision of more tangible support during their day-to-day activities at the university, a number of positive experiences were shared. Out of the five participants, four had applied for and received support from the university, though one of those four did so in the role of a PhD student rather than as a member of staff. The support they received ranged from access to accessible technologies to lowering a part of their workload, which had most negatively interacted with their impairment. When asked how they felt about the support they received, all four were generally positive, with one participant remarking that "if in my earlier career I was given what I have now . . . then my career would be very different." In particular, the participant felt that the university department dealing with accessible technology ably supported two of the participants and received significant and justifiable praise for their work:

> He [the officer working in the department] was the one person who has helped me the most. Not just in practical terms, but you could see that he was a person who could understand what I was going through. And so that's also important, because sometimes you get what you need done but it's hard to see the personal side . . . so sometimes it's

important that you can see someone understands what you're going through.

The importance of similar relationships with line managers and mentors was also reified and referred to as important sources of personal support as well as, alongside the union, a potential source of knowledge about rights and accommodations. While some of these accommodations were accessed without difficulty, the long process of forms, evidence, and meetings, on top of the extra work that the participants had to do to remain invisible, was felt to be a burdensome responsibility. This was particularly the case where, to gain support in mobility and typing, the participants ended up having to go to meetings and type out long forms.

In addition, the participants felt that they had a shared origin in individual action with others with similar diagnoses, in response to their environments not being fully accessible. In other words, the responsibility for minimizing the effects of their impairments was placed on other people with disabilities. While this seems to be typical of disability support systems at universities in the UK (Ewens et al. 2011), four of the participants would have preferred a more "visible" and "proactive" support system where everyday practices were accessible to a broader range of people and impairments without requiring extra accommodations, while also making those extra accommodations and how to access them common knowledge. For example, one participant who had mobility issues did not know that priority parking was an option for a significant period.

> The ideal situation, as someone who works on curricula, would be that we wouldn't put in place fixes for disability so to speak, prostheses, instead we would teach in a manner that, regardless of anyone in the class who has x, y, or z, is accessible.

There were also several flaws in the support offered to a number of participants in the study. The most common flaw was that, when compared to students with disabilities, staff with disabilities were felt to require lower quality support and remain less visible. For instance, one participant said that "if a staff member has an issue, I think it gets deprioritized compared to a student issue," something she felt was due to the status of students as a source of income. Similarly, another participant was aware of the details of the support offered to disabled students by the Disabled Students Allowance and the university disability service but thought that staff would "have to sort it out [themselves]. By sort out, I mean figuring out who you had to talk to about what." An important addendum to these feelings of lower value to the university was that both participants believed that once they did find the appropriate source, then an appropriate range of support became available.

The physical campus of the university was twice noted as being "not particularly friendly" and was seen as a potential barrier, by discouraging future disabled students or staff from applying to the university and by causing physical access issues and obstacles. One participant also said she faced issues accessing the support prescribed by their personal National Health Service specialists when the university's occupational health assessor believed a different form of treatment would be more appropriate. This was despite the prescribed condition not being in the university specialist's focus of expertise; consequently, the National Health Service treatment was eventually shown to be the better of the two conditions and was eventually administered. However, this advice was only acted on after the research participant rejected the alternative treatment suggested by the occupational health assessor, putting the participant in an unfortunate position with their employers.

One participant was also concerned that other advice about nonmedical issues could lead to inappropriate treatment or support, which could worsen the effects of a staff member's impairment or their ability to effectively perform their role. Instead, the participant recommended that the university be more mindful of the areas of expertise of the occupational health assessors and deploy them accordingly, as well as ensuring better treatment of staff during their assessment periods. While neither the participants nor the primary researcher was in the position to show such an intervention at the time of the study, the examples each of them provided were still demonstrative of the type of additional pressures that could be placed on academics with impairments.

Finally, it was also felt that the reduction of certain duties that were affected by participants' impairment, while praised, was still a source of concern for a number of them. For instance, one participant felt that they required a complete cessation of those duties, and thus they were not sure that the university would be willing to accommodate that desire considering the importance of their role. The effects of their impairment had progressed to such an extent that if the university would or could not agree to an enhanced course of support then "that will be making me leave [the university and academic career]." This would have represented an emotional as well as a vocational schism, they felt, as they still enjoyed being successful in the other aspects of their role. Eventually, it was a particularly complicated situation that was still in the process of being resolved during the study, and one in which the nature of a career had to be weighed against the rights of the individual.

The issues that this study identified

Analysis of the data recorded during the interviews identified two *core categories of issues* that academics with disabilities experienced at the university: ableism and the construction of the social issues surrounding disability.

These two issues are now discussed in further detail later, followed by a discussion of the implication and issues of policy and methodology that this study identified.

Ableism and constructions of disability

The theme of "identity" that emerged in the findings was focused on how the participants viewed and defined themselves as disabled or not. The participants did not construct themselves as less able or willing than able-bodied academics, except in situations where the effects of their impairment were not accounted for. Therefore, the theme of identity did not contain ableism. The theme of disclosure and academic culture and its relation to ableism can be split into three subsections: internal ableism, fear of encountering ableism, and ableism resulting from disclosure. The reluctance to disclose could originate in internal ableism, but other comments about colleagues' potential reactions supported the notion that ableism comes from the fear of encountering ableism if the participant disclosed. Although this fear was not the case in the findings as there were no incidences of ableism resulting from disclosure, the lack of a feeling that it would be the case points to a culture that does not welcome disability or difference.

The participants also felt that the university culture of standards and promotion metrics can be ableist and possibly in violation of all the requirements of the 2010 Equality Act. For example, to fulfill the metrics and advance their careers, academics are obliged to buy into a paradigm that privileges constant engagement and availability. As the often-invisible effects of impairment make overworking difficult, even threatening physical and mental health, and universities had not managed to minimize their impact in the era of the study (Williams and Marvin 2015), the overworking paradigm privileged *able-bodiedness*. In addition, the participants felt that the blame for not reaching the standards was explicitly located in the individual, as the standards were viewed as value-neutral and not engaging with other values. In addition, it was felt that reaching for these standards was couched in the wording that implied it was an individual's choice to strive for these values. Thus, it was also felt that these standards discriminated against anyone who had any commitments other than their academic post.

The university's perceived culture of secrecy surrounding issues of disability and mental health and its culture of "not-admitting-to-struggling with the demands of academic life" was also felt to be interrelated by participants and contained characteristics of ableism. This ableism was linked to the pressure the participants felt to be "an ideal academic" to conform to the professionalized culture of *the university* and to be seen as competent and self-reliant (Morrissey 2015). Alone, this finding would not be characterized as ableist, but the effects of the participants' impairments and disabilities put additional pressures on their standing, particularly when compared to the standing of nondisabled colleagues. These effects were not accounted for in the measures of competence outlined by the university. When the interaction of the environment with impairment effects requires them to request accommodations, disabled academics lose the ability to remain invisible and competent. The culture of silence even makes the disabled academics who remain invisible complicit in the ableism experienced by themselves and others.

The flaws experienced in the support offered by the university led all the participants being placed in an "adversarial position" (Devlin and Pothier 2006), where their choice moved between registering as biomedically disabled with the university to being unable to perform their role. This concept is considered ableist by Wolbring (2008), particularly when, as occurred with two of the participants with chronic pain, the effects of their impairment were impactful but not diagnosed. Further evidence of ableism was also visible in the process for accessing accommodations and the assumption that these accommodations were the responsibility of the disabled person themselves, which was something referred to previously as *responsibilization* (Rose 1999). The process was also designed in such a manner as to assume that academics should have the ability to type effectively, accurately and without pain, and to attend required assessment meetings at generally given times. As the requests for accommodation for typing software and priority parking attest, this should not have been assumed.

It can be argued that there was sufficient evidence from the participants' testimony to suggest that there was ableism in the university. The most explicit constructions of disability identified through this research into the university's practices were its individualized and biomedicalized construction of support services. To access these services, the participants were required to disclose their diagnoses and then have their needs assessed, meaning that these needs were constructed from a starting point of medically impaired bodies, with the solution being access to accommodations on an individual level. This process appears to match Oliver's (1996) original characterization of the individual model of disability and its inherent weaknesses. In this case, the societal barriers that were experienced by the participants, for example, the inaccessibility of parts of the campus, could not be addressed.

This being said, it also appeared that the participants did not internalize the more discriminatory assumptions of Oliver's individual model of disability, that of disability being a deficit and people with disabilities as having experienced a tragedy (Tremain 2015). Instead, they held their own definitions, which, while they did include individual experiences of impairment, also understood disability to be a "difference," which could even add to their competence in certain areas of life. Indeed, by doing so they can be said to be exercising "technologies of the self" (Foucault 1988); that is to say, power exercised by the individual, on the individual, which can empower the individual.

So, what was taken from this study that can inform future directions of emancipatory participatory research?

Conclusion

The primary weakness of this form of emancipatory participatory study arose from its nature as a small-scale, qualitative research project, which was limited by the power to achieve any direct outcomes. As was the case with Waterfield et al. (2018), this lack of time and power resulted in the sample not being large enough or representative enough to provide the form of evidence, which could be valued by policy makers (Vaccaro et al. 2014). Although this project did manage to fulfill Waterfield et al.'s (2018) request for a study with an immediate context by being in a single university, doing so compromised the ability to explore the potential impact of intersectional factors. It also conceded the possibility of representing the data from each participant as shown by Williams and Marvin (2015).

In addition, the exploration of the immediate context of the university was limited by the time constraints of an MRes degree, with the research and dissertation having to be completed over a summer semester. The research therefore did not provide any opportunity to investigate other influential factors, such as university-specific policies on the construction of disability at the university, nor their impacts on the disabled academics who worked there.

The final weakness of this type of emancipatory participatory projects is that despite originating in and being designed to attempt to create a positive impact on the environment of academics at the university and produce findings, which demonstrated that the environment of the university contains instances of ableism, this research possibly can possibly have little visible impact. Any potential impact that can take place after submission of the project is often left without evaluation, and even if it does take place, it is often difficult to create a valid system of measurement to assess it. Ideally, therefore, similar future research should include a plan for impact assessment, possibly by following up on the recipients of the findings to see if any action had been taken as a result and by planning time before the end of the project for this action to take place.

However, despite the limitations of this study, this research revealed that the experiences of the participants, that is to say academics who are disabled and employed by the University of Bath at the time of writing, included instances of ableism and made a number of recommendations to address this matter. In addition, the project made a theoretical contribution to research on academics with disabilities by providing further evidence that these academics often faced disadvantage and discrimination and by attempting to explore the discursive construction of disability at a single university. In this respect, it talked truth to power and thus had its own internal validity.

4 Case study of a large-scale museums-based project

Simon Hayhoe, Helena Garcia Carrisoza, Jonathan Rix, Kieron Sheehy, and Jane Seale

Introduction

In this chapter, we examine a museum access project called ARCHES, which used an emancipatory paradigm and participatory methodology to inform arts technologies and information in an effort to make cultural heritage in Europe more accessible—again, in this chapter, this will be referred to as emancipatory participatory methodology for convenience. The aim of the project was to empower emancipatory participatory groups to co-develop their own research practice and take ownership of their groups and then to use this research practice to co-design and test museum technologies and learning strategies.

It was the objective of the project to inform more democratic museums for visitors with what are traditionally called sensory and learning disabilities and to support museums and technologies companies in their own participatory practice. Importantly, the participants in the project were first and foremost a group of self-selecting people with sensory and learning disabilities, and then technology professionals and engineers, museum professionals, and volunteers and academics.

As was argued in Chapter 2, this case study demonstrates that the current system of institutional power and funding make what can be termed *pure* emancipatory participatory research unmanageable. The project itself was funded by a large grant, and, as a compromise that lessened the participatory nature of the project, this grant had to be administered by the consortium of research and development organizations, universities, and seven museums in London, Madrid, Vienna, and Oviedo in northern Spain.

Thus, and in common with other studies that are administered by highly technical funding strategies, although the project was based on emancipatory participatory methodology, it could not claim to have used a pure emancipatory participatory methodology. More particularly, the partners also developed this study in the first instance, had drafted a full proposal,

DOI: 10.4324/9781003083924-4

A large museums-based project 41

and appointed a separate advisory board of academics from universities that weren't directly involved in the participatory practice. This should be borne in mind when reading this chapter and evaluating its methods.

The context of the project

The road to emancipatory participatory methodology in the arts, creative cultures, and museums can be placed in a historical context of inclusion, and, according to Axel (2018), this practice has passed through three eras. The first era, from the end of the eighteenth century until the middle of the twentieth century, was that of teachers breaking with tradition and accepting the abilities of their students. However, as was the fashion of the time, these teachers worked with people with disabilities separately, reinforcing difference through segregated environments, while at the same time disabled people were rarely listened to themselves. Furthermore, in this era, the prevailing thinking was that each person's needs were linked to their ability to enjoy or appreciate the arts. Consequently, throughout their careers, people with disabilities and their teachers were rarely recognized as developing a high-level understanding of personal intellectual development.

The second era of this access and inclusion, which began in the second half of the twentieth century, was that of scientists starting to challenge the accessible practices of art institutions, schools, colleges, and museums. These scientists suggested that what was thought to be inaccessible to people because of sensory or cognitive impairments could be taught through different sensory combinations or alternative learning strategies. Many of these access issues were felt to be simple challenges that could be solved through what is now termed the deficit model (Harry and Klingner 2007). Moreover, these scientists showed that the sensory properties of objects were not restricted to those with the *full* use of their senses and their cognitive ability. Instead, it was found that objects and concepts taught in cultural institutions could have alternative information properties and could be interpreted by various sensory and cognitive mechanisms.

According to Axel, an increasing body of contemporary museums and galleries are finally undergoing a third era of access and inclusion and developing a growing acceptance of what was once thought to be radical thinking as mainstream thinking. Hence, many cultural institutions offer accessible art classes, inclusive technologies and tools, such as accessible audio descriptions, wheelchairs, and signers, in mainstream galleries and not just through separate routes and tours. For example, Axel's own organization, Art Beyond Sight, provides drawing sets for people with visual impairments on request for use in regular museum art classes. Similarly, at the time of writing other organizations, such as ONCE (Spain), the RNID/

42 *A large museums-based project*

Action on Hearing Loss (UK), SignTime (Austria), and the V&A (UK) had inclusive activities organized by people with disabilities themselves. It was within this latter context that our emancipatory research project, ARCHES, was developed.

As I mentioned earlier, ARCHES aimed to create inclusive European museums for adults with access needs, such as sensory impairment and learning difficulties, through the analysis and development of apps, access strategies, and visitor experiences. Following on from this emancipatory participatory research practice, ARCHES participants co-created technologies such as apps and touch devices and critiqued and wrote access policies and practices. The six museums involved in ARCHES were the Victoria and Albert Museum (V&A) and the Wallace Collection in London, Kunst Historisches Museum (KHM) in Vienna, Thyssen-Bornemisza Museum (the Thyssen) and Lázaro Galdiano Museum (the Lázaro Galdiano) in Madrid, and Bellas Artes Museum (Bellas Artes) in Oviedo. In addition, the project involved two university partners, University of Bath and the Open University, and five technical partners Vr-Vis and Signtime in Vienna, Treelogic in Oviedo, ArteConTacto in Barcelona, and Coprix Media in Belgrade, Serbia. To develop its participatory practice, ARCHES's held weekly and then fortnightly group consultations, meetings, presentations, and discussions over the course of two years in four groups, one each in Vienna, London, Madrid, and Oviedo, with each of these sessions being hosted by the museums.

The initial ARCHES sessions began in early 2017 with the creation of pilot group sessions in London, with participants from local disability groups and associations, the two participating universities, and the museums themselves. This group aimed to have a working membership of 25 adults, although the initial number was much higher and then fluctuated over the following years between around 50 and 10 at any one time, depending on the commitments of the members. Over the course of the following two years, several members also decided not to continue for a number of different reasons, including frustrations with the process, what they believed the technologies should include and other members of the groups. Six months after beginning the London sessions, group sessions were then organized in Madrid, Vienna, and Oviedo based on the same model by taking on the experiences of these initial London sessions. This phased development of the group sessions was largely for practical reasons, as it was felt that lessons could be learned from the initial London sessions that would make forming the other three cities' sessions smoother and less risky. Such a large, coordinated emancipatory participatory project had never happened in these European museums before, and so it was felt that this tentative approach was prudent.

To ensure a range of experiences in the sessions, over the course of the two years, adults with disabilities were invited to participate through contacts with a broad range of local adult services or providers of support for adults in their respective cities. However, beyond these invitations and the local nature of these providers, no sampling was conducted of these participants, as it was felt that participants should never be excluded if they had experiences to share. In addition, each of the museums involved in ARCHES appointed a research team coordinator to bring together and enable the research team membership, which eased the working practices of each group. In addition, this museum coordinator organized visits from the technologists, engineers, and academics and helped the groups identify manageable and meaningful aims for new technologies. The overall goal of this group dynamic was to ensure the development and the assessment of the new technologies as they arose and to situate the participants at the heart of the research and co-design the process through an ebb and flow of new discussions and challenges.

The development of the sessions

Over the course of the following two years, the groups also collaborated with the technical partners in charge of the development of applications and tools as well as professionals at the museums. Initially, the London-based emancipatory participatory research group worked over a six-month period to develop their code of ethics and ways of working, and their processes and findings were then shared with the museums in other cities to provide a starting point for the development of their groups. In addition, after six months of emancipatory participatory sessions, professionals from the partner museums received training in the development of emancipatory participatory research during a two-day session in Madrid that ensured that all of the groups coordinated their approaches to ethics and data gathering.

By its nature, working with these disparate groups of participants needed an iterative and idiosyncratic approach to the development and testing of the technologies and learning strategies as they were brought to fruition. Consequently, to support and provide structure for the sessions, ARCHES drew on the framework for the design and evaluation of mobile applications developed by Shoukry et al. (2015), and the data analysis was carried out using a grounded methodology-based approach (Hayhoe 2012, 2020). This grounded methodology approach was based on three stages of qualitative analysis: the first being an open coding phase, in which initial issues and variables were identified by participants in the project; the second being an axial coding phase, during which these issues and variables were studied in greater detail, and their importance was evaluated for their level of importance and an initial hypothesis was formulated; and the third being the selective coding phase, during which the initial hypothesis was tested against new data, and a refined analysis was developed in partnership with the participants.

The ARCHES sessions also looked at the feasibility of creating a web platform, interactive and multi-media touch technologies, a sign language avatar and an app for smartphones and tablets, and several on-site activities with the final purpose of making museums more accessible for people with sensory and learning disabilities. During these sessions, different options were also considered to collect already-existing digital resources in the field of art such as making use of the existing software platforms released by different European organizations, including Europeana and the Rijksmuseum in Amsterdam. These platforms provide direct types of approaches to access artworks in different formats, from images to 3D models together with videos, text, and audio tracks. Furthermore, mainstream websites, such as Art Project by the Google Cultural Institute, WikiArt, and DBpedia, were also considered and used as a starting point for the co-design of ARCHES software. However, as there was a limit to the amount of material that was digitized and currently available from these sources at the time, ARCHES sessions also explored alternative apps and hardware developed by the participating museums, such as those recorded for audio guides. The aim of this exploration was thus to make as many accessible images, touchable models, and descriptions of artworks available through apps and unique forms of hardware via the Web via mobile phones and tablets while they visited the museums.

The basis of this technical approach was also designed to introduce participants to new and state-of-the-art technologies, such as augmented reality, avatars, relief printers and models, context-sensitive tactile audio guides, and digital data and image processing techniques. In this framework, museums played an important role in this process by adapting content and reinterpreting their artworks in ways that were most suitable for all visitors in partnership with the participants. Consequently, the emancipatory participatory sessions also focused on developing, testing, and ensuring different forms of communication within and between other participants in different cities, and stimulated cross-border collaboration to address common exclusion and challenges in their cities.

This chapter now reflects on the experiences and practices of these participants over the course of two years of sessions. It is written as a realistic overview of what we felt we achieved, given the availability of inclusive practices and technologies, the constraints we worked within, and a reflection of how we had to compromise participatory practice.

The approach to using emancipatory participatory methodology

The design of the methodology

As we mentioned earlier, the methodology used for ARCHES was a combination of participatory practice and grounded methodology, which was adapted to analyze the use of technologies and tools in cultural institutions through three phases of practice (Hayhoe 2020). The participatory practice used during ARCHES was informed by a contemporary understanding of the emancipatory paradigm, which was designed to engage participants in the examination of their own inclusion and access needs through self-advocacy and agency (White et al. 2010). Subsequently, forms of participatory practice were implemented in partner museums by actively involving participants in the decision-making and design processes. In addition, participants were asked to suggest possible uses and the contexts of uses of the technologies developed by partners.

Importantly, the work at hand was conducted using a nonclassificatory approach to access preferences (Rix 2007; Hayhoe 2019). This approach was the result of the observation that no two people have exactly the same preferences, that people should not be classified according to what are thought to be single impairments or disabilities—for example, participants should not be identified as solely "sensory impaired" or "learning disabled"—and that everyone can be assumed to have an access preference of one form or another even if it is in a mild form. The assumption that all people have access preferences also meant that during ARCHES, technology, academic, and museum partners were also found to have access preferences themselves. Therefore, their voices in the development of technologies and inclusion in the museum based on their own personal experience were seen as being equally valid as those who were recruited because of their access preferences.

As we mentioned earlier, the participant groups met in the partner museums in London, Madrid, Vienna, and Oviedo, from 2017 to 2019. These participant groups started with up to 50 attendees—usually the first meetings—although these numbers dropped off during the course of the project, with some attendees coming for some sessions and not others, while others attended only a few sessions and then stopped coming. It was noted that this drop in attendance was often related to people's pressure of work, getting new jobs or engaging in new or alternative activities; however, others did not state their reason for leaving, and a small number left because they felt their access preferences were not being met. Despite this fluctuation in attendance, a core group of 20 or more participants attended sessions regularly in all four cities.

Data collection methods

During the project, data were collected through formal consultation with the groups on issues such as technological developments and use, interviews with participants, sound recording of sessions and tours, visual methods, art-making tasks, participant observation diaries and personal diaries, systematic literature reviews, topical reviews based on less formal literature searches and logs recorded by the participants. It was also noted that over the course of the session, participants increasingly made their own notes either on their mobile devices or using traditional pen and notebooks, and these were often shared with the participants and used to inform co-design tasks. As part of its communication strategy, and at the request of participants, the London group also employed a scribe for people with hearing access preferences who requested written information. This scribe sat next to people who requested "subtitling" of the spoken conversation, and these data were also available as formal written data for use by the participant researchers.

To evaluate the participatory practice, interviews were also conducted during the latter stages of the emancipatory participatory groups and pilot testing. The interviews were conducted by experienced field researchers. As a result, it was felt that the emancipatory participatory nature of the research was compromised, but this was unavoidable as these interviews were a requirement of the project's funders. During this evaluation, three of the researchers who had regularly attended groups in three of the four different cities interviewed participants from these cities, while another researcher interviewed participants from the technology partners. With the exception of the technology partners, who were interviewed via videolink, all the group interviews were conducted face to face, and interviews were recorded electronically using tablets, smartphones, or laptops—the apps used on the tablets, laptops, and telephones included Evernote and QuickTime.

In each of the cities, the following participants were interviewed: One supporter from the group, who was a regular attender and who supported other participants through activities such as signing, translating, and providing material help with mobility or similar; one facilitator, who was a participant who helped develop the groups, assisting with recruitment and developing exercises; five participants with what were traditionally thought to have access preferences or impairments, and diary keepers; one or two museum research coordinators from each city; a director of one museum per city if they were available; and an education or access manager per city if they were available. In addition, one of the interviewers conducted an interview with the research associate involved in the project, who was also seen as a participant. Interviewees from the technology partners included the following participants from each company: two developers or engineers per company and one manager per company.

As the interviewers were native English speakers, and in an effort to coordinate interviews with the various partners, it was decided to subcontract interpreters in Spain and Austria. In addition, to provide structure for the interviews, it was also decided to base the evaluation questions on six validities: *Intersubjective validity*, for instance, participants were asked, Is the project credible and meaningful to you? *Contextual validity*, for instance, participants were asked, Is ARCHES relevant to the local situation? *Participatory validity*, for instance, participants were asked, Is this project allowing you to play a full and active part in the research process? *Catalytic validity*, for instance, participants were asked, Is ARCHES creating opportunities for social action? *Ethical validity*, for instance, participants were asked, Do you think this project is sound and just in what it is trying to achieve and the way it is trying to achieve it? *Empathic validity*, for instance, participants were asked, Is this project increasing empathy among participants? Wherever possible, during the interviews and if it was felt that the question was appropriate to the particular interviewee, participants were also asked the following questions: Where you are and where you have been in relation to issues of access? What activities have you been undertaking with the emancipatory participatory groups? What activities have people struggled with and thought successful? What impact has ARCHES had on you? What are your plans to act upon lessons learned from ARCHES?

As with all research, the data collection worked within certain constraints and, as with all projects, there were issues that affected the ability to collect data in a uniform manner. These constraints included the following issues:

1 The project was conducted in a limited number of museums, which had their own organizational cultures and diverse European cultures. In addition, the museums also had existing styles of providing access, rooms, and exhibitions that could be made available to the ARCHES project, which made it impossible for us to claim the group sessions were wholly consistent.
2 The museums worked within the normal financial constraints of contemporary public institutions and had to account for their time carefully with a finite number of staff.
3 The museums were mainly art museums, and although some visits were made to alternative museums, such as science museums, the focus on the findings was largely limited to artworks alone.
4 Three of the four participant groups were in capital cities. Furthermore, five of the six host museums could be considered to be "national museums" or "national collections," that is to say, museums funded directly by the state. This meant that when developing a picture of "museum access," it was not possible to generalize about other specialized cultural

sites, such as specialist museums, monuments, and religious buildings, although Oviedo provided useful data on regionality.

The findings from the participatory practice

In all of the cities and museums involved in the project, there seemed to be two sides to participation, with some tensions emerging between the professionals and the participants with disabilities, and between groups of people with what they felt were different disabilities. What now follows is a discussion of these issues, which we identified during our evaluation, which are split into their six respective validities.

Intersubjective validity

The intersubjective validity questions generated a number of positive responses during the interviews and was adjudged to be one of the strongest elements of participation during ARCHES. The museum staff in particular felt that their participation added to their skills-base and knowledge of participants. During the course of the emancipatory participatory groups, even the most experienced staff seemed to find something that increased their knowledge, particularly their experiences of working with people whose access preferences they had not previously come across. Moreover, because the emancipatory participatory sessions were stretched out over the course of over two years, a number of museum professionals said that they were able to delve into issues they had come across before but in greater detail.

Similarly, one museum professional said that she found the project raised awareness of a range of different challenges that many museum visitors faced. This issue had come as somewhat of a surprise, as at first she had previously worked with visitors with a range of disabilities in her museum and felt this experience was transferable to ARCHES. For instance, before ARCHES, she said she felt as if she had a "fairly good grip" on access issues, but over the course of two years, she had realized, "it's been enlightening, it's also been a bit terrifying and it's been enjoyable and it's been frustrating, but it's definitely been meaningful." Similar feelings of hard-won understanding were also expressed by professionals from a number of the partner technology companies. For example, one technology professional felt it was particularly interesting to work with people from museums, as it helped him gain an insight into the way they thought about access. Furthermore, similar sentiments were also discussed about working with the academic partners. "But here again, [ARCHES] has a strong academic part and I like it. Because I liked university, I like science. I think this is a very good way to see and analyse the world."

A large museums-based project 49

For a number of participants with stronger access preferences, two forms of need seemed to be fulfilled more than others during the course of the sessions: first, there was a feeling that all the participants were a productive part of a live project, had an important part to play in the group sessions, were a productive part of broader society, and were recognized by the museum, universities, and technology companies as having human value; second, a number of participants felt that their voices had led to a form of inclusive activity, some form of tangible change, and it was this change that provided self-esteem. Furthermore, numerous participants with access preferences stated a need to learn, a need to feel part of a group or a social movement, and a social need to meet with friends and to feel a part of a community. Through the group activities and active practice, participants with more significant access preferences also saw the need to feel the partner museums were a place to look forward to visiting.

For instance, one participant felt that the sessions had allowed him to gain access to the Kunsthistorisches Museum, somewhere he had not been to before, and to familiarize himself with exhibitions and follow guided tours, which he would not normally have considered following. Furthermore, these visits had helped him to shape access he had not previously considered and activated a need to develop inclusion in the museum. As he said, "I want barriers to disappear, I want there to be more accessibility and I want museums to be inclusive and I'm someone who can contribute to this."

For many of those participants who felt they were making a difference, it was also important to develop intellectual and critical skills during the course of the groups, which in turn led to a sense of self-esteem and achievement. Some participants took this aspect of the group further and, acting on their own initiative, attempted to undertake their own exercises after individual sessions had finished. For instance, one participant described a self-directed exercise after a museum session had ended, something that could add to their understanding of inclusive practice and add to the purpose of the project.

> Afterwards, we all dispersed. I stayed on at the museum and I done a little mystery shopper of my own. It's fantastic, you can go to the information desk for information, you can ask them [if] they have an iPad. They will put it straight on to BSL [British Sign Language]. Up pops the little man and he signs everywhere.

There were, however, instances where participant sessions did not seem to satisfy intersubjective needs. Reasons cited by participants were largely those of a lack of technology appearing, technology not being developed in a timely manner or the participants feeling that they were not intellectually or professionally stimulated by the tasks during the sessions—this was a hard balance as the attendants had a range of what they felt were personal achievements. In other instances, people attended because they were interested in technology but had little interest in the museums themselves or in the artworks that the sessions covered. For example, one participant discussed sessions where she felt presenters had just come along because they were sent by the museum, talked about a personal interest they had, and then left. It was as if these presenters had little "buy in" to the project, which left participants feeling demotivated and slightly disappointed about attending. As she stated:

> I think there was one about a design museum or an exhibition about something and the lady came in and did a presentation and it was quite complicated. I think a lot of it went over the participants' heads, and they left, and it wasn't linked to an active project that we were doing.

In other recorded instances, there were tensions between participants with different access preferences and different levels of experience in delivering or advising on access themselves. For instance, some participants were particularly frustrated that their expertise was not recognized, and they were not remunerated for their time, and as in previous roles, they had been employed as access professionals. In addition, some participants felt that the speed of the sessions was often too slow and paced toward the slowest learners.

> A project which aims at addressing all sorts of disabilities at once reduces persons with disabilities to being disabled. A real emancipatory participatory project would bring together, for example, people with cognitive disabilities and journalists or blind persons and architects. Disabilities are not an amorph something which is just "other than normal." There is a great variety inside disability which has to be respected in order to meet the people's individual strengths and disability-related needs. Combining blind people and people with cognitive disabilities in a series of workshops leads to boring hours without occupation for both sides, since the contents these two groups can work on are often different.
> The one-and-for-all tool for people with disabilities does not exist and will never exist. A good example is the game in the app which can now—after months and months—be played with VoiceOver output, but which is no fun for non-seeing people.
> (Personal Communication from Members of Vienna Group to VRVis)

Contextual validity

The interviews with the participants seemed to highlight a particularly important correlation between contextual and catalytic validities to such an extent that it was almost felt they could be the same category. In addition, there was a general agreement between the participants that their local communities could gain from developing emancipatory participatory groups. Many of the regular members of the sessions thought that ARCHES could lead to a change in their local communities, talking about aspirations such as the modification of information and improvements to public transport that could be developed through their sessions. In contrast, the museum professionals mentioned more concrete contextual changes that could come about, based on their previous experiences of their own work in this field. These changes often related to practicalities, the size of the museums, and the ability to link like-minded institutions rather than local cultural issues beyond the museums partnering in the project. This led to a large degree of enthusiasm by participants with more significant access needs.

> It's what we're doing, we're going to make the museum more accessible to people with disabilities whether they have a learning disability or whether they're deaf or partially deaf, or blind or partially blind, deaf/blind, so we're looking into all that.

Furthermore, a number of participants felt that ARCHES helped individual museums develop unique technologies they would not normally be able to afford as a collective. Other participants felt that the project could bridge a gap between large and small museums, allowing for diverse participatory experiences. For example, it was felt that combining two very different museums, the relatively small Museo Lazaro Galdiano and the larger national Museo Thyssen, benefitted both parties. For instance, Lazaro Galdiano managed to focus more on the human dimension of participation and Museo Thyssen managed to work with different forms of art and craft. As one participant put it, "The combination of these two museums has given the project a fuller perspective."

Similar sentiments were expressed by other museum professionals. For example, a participant from the Wallace Collection felt both the Wallace and the V&A could learn from each other and forge stronger, long-term links. This was particularly important for the Wallace Collection, who could not normally afford expensive custom-built technologies for access purposes, as it was a smaller, specialist collection. As one of the participants from this collection stated, they normally would be in a pragmatic position "where we can't really afford to put money into developing any kind of new tech or new audiences, let alone our underrepresented audiences." Participants from all four groups also felt that ARCHES could help local institutions and particularly make local communities more aware of disability access and disability rights. However, this said, for these participants, the notion of helping and raising awareness in the local community seemed a little more like an abstract vision for the future, rather than something that could happen immediately. Consequently, during the interviews, few could give specific examples where they could see specific immediate changes happening beyond these broad aspirations.

Participatory validity

On a local level, there appeared to be what was considered to be a good degree of participation within the group, and many participants provided colorful illustrations of their group participation during the interviews. The participants also felt that they were heard by other participants in the group on the whole, and the coordinators and participants appeared to form a strong bond with each other over the course of two years. However, it was also mentioned that simply bonding with those who ran the group was not enough to feel a sense of participation.

Of greater importance to the participants was the need to feel that what was being discussed during group sessions was acted upon, or at least what they told the professional partners could lead to future action. In this respect, being listened to and providing some evidence of inclusion in an output seemed to be linked with a sense of feeling valued in the minds of the participants. For instance, participants in both Spanish cities felt that when they gave feedback, it was generally acted upon, there was a viable and observable change in the following days after they expressed their views, and their activities came from ideas generated by the groups themselves. Participants also generally recognized that coordinators put in a great deal of hard work outside the sessions to make them interesting, and they had not been blocked when their opinions were offered.

> He [the participant] thinks he's being listened to within the project and he actually thinks that the participants are protagonists of the project, so he feels like they are really being listened to in order to improve the conditions of accessibility within the Museo.

A number of participants also said that the groups also ended up feeling like a family and participants often said that they made many friends during the course of the study despite not expecting to do so when the sessions began. Furthermore, a number of participants felt the group coordinators were flexible, dedicated, and had driven the project forward. To comply with their objectives, several participants said that a number of outcomes had been set prior to activities, and these outcomes helped to focus their input in the project.

> So, of course, we are not only listened to. Our ideas, suggestions and works are not only taken into consideration but it's the only way that the project is working, because if we couldn't do that the project wouldn't have started.

Many of the museum professionals also felt as if their participation was appreciated and their voices heard during the course of the sessions. A number of these professionals stated that it did not just as feel if they themselves were doing their job or going through *the motions* because they were paid to attend. The professionals stated that they also felt valued for what they did, they felt good about what they had achieved in individual sessions, and they had built lasting relationships with colleagues and the participants recruited for their access preferences. A number of professional participants also felt that, although it was tough working with other professionals from other disciplines with different expectations and different narratives, the effort and difficulty were worth it in the end. Even the postponement or lack of some technologies to test the technologies during some sessions appeared to provide a sense of resilience among the regular attenders.

> It's been interesting to work with them [other professionals] too, even though there's been problems and delays . . . but they're all incredibly dedicated and understand what it is we're trying to do I think on the whole and have tried very, very hard to understand issues of participants.

However, although some of the regular participants felt as if their voices were being valued, a number of the participants felt excluded at different points in the project, lessening their participatory validity. In particular, some participants believed that their colleagues' voices were overvalued or at least valued more than theirs within the group. In other instances, a number of participants felt intimated by others in the session, as they seemed more confident, forceful, and even egotistical. In addition, it was found that some museum professional participants did not feel valued, largely because they felt they were following a route map they had not helped to construct—most notably they felt the academic partners had developed the methodology almost independently of their own rythmns and needs. In other instances, participants were unsure of their role in the group and, as a number of the technologies had not appeared as quickly as they expected them to, tensions occurred in the group about what activities they could do while they waited. This led to some museum professionals feeling a lesser sense of fulfillment in an ownership of the project and to a feeling that their participation was being tinged by a sense of omission. For others, there was a feeling that the workload ARCHES produced left them unable to fulfill their other professional duties, as at some points over the two years, the demands of the other participants were all encompassing. For instance, one museum professional said that they felt constrained and had to leave decisions to others in the museum.

> It's been hard in that me and [Co-Worker] split one day a week on ARCHES, other people work full time and that, for me, it's created a problem in that . . . I have two other massive programs that I run, this is a tiny part.

Over the two years, there were also instances of participants who stopped coming to the sessions, and it was not clear why they had stopped. In other instances, participants said that others had stopped coming because they had been asked to work with technologies that weren't in their native language or had adapted settings that hadn't been adjusted beforehand, so some participants who were less skilled in the use of technology felt *a priori* excluded. Other participants also felt that there was a gap among their aims, the universities' aims, and the technology partners' aims, with other participants also feeling that there was a hierarchy of participants being imposed on them. As some regular attenders in the sessions wrote:

> The project was made up of some companies' project ideas which had been developed before the project started. The persons with disabilities had the role of testers, but we had no influence at all on the development. A project which excludes people with disabilities from its development will never be able to meet these persons' needs and cannot be labelled participatory.

> Time is precious, even to persons with disabilities. And expertise is precious, life-based and rare expertise is even more so. The ARCHES project demanded the expertise of people with disabilities. Three hours every two or three weeks for more than a year—without any form of remuneration. I felt that the project workers in Vienna (khm, vrvis) appreciated our expertise very much, but I missed any respect for my time and my expertise in the project design.
>
> (Personal Communication from Members of Vienna Group to VRVis)

Catalytic validity

There appeared to be correlation between contextual and catalytic validities, with the contextual validities being reported in a more concrete way during the interviews. However, there was a general sense of optimism among many of the participants and a general feeling that even small changes, such as video projects, would lead to a greater understanding of accessibility because of the project. There was also mention in a number of the interviews with participants with greater access needs that ARCHES could possibly change the public's perceptions of access and inclusion over time.

Furthermore, catalytic validities were frequently also closely correlated with empathetic validities during the interviews or at least a number of regular participants expressed a sense of empathy with other participants they met over the course of the sessions. It was also felt that small changes in practice after attending the groups could help develop a momentum at an institutional level and lead to more significant external institutional changes. For example, one of the museum professionals felt that tangible resources and their promotion often helped to disseminate the idea of access and equality better than traditional projects. Furthermore, they told us that the effect of promoting technologies was often exponential as, when resources such as bigger signs explaining pictures and audio guides were used in real life settings, there was a marked increase in visitors with access needs. For instance, it was felt that others saw accessible issues up-close and museum visitors saw accessible resources as normal.

Indirect catalytic practice was also thought to be significant and could lead to a further understanding of access and inclusion issues among the different cities' sessions. For example, one professional seemed to be proud that she had helped to develop a new professionally produced video that was uploaded to at least one museum's website. This website, the participant felt, helped the group gain recognition among casual viewers of the website, making people with disabilities seem part of a very "visible" group and giving disability a sense of cultural and institutional recognition.

> The video presentation and all the resources available, will achieve a normalization of the disability.... So, the social impact has to be done with this type of littlest stones, littlest steps, but that will make sense at the end of the day.

Similar catalysts were described by the technology partners who felt that their practice in future projects could be positively affected by their experiences in ARCHES. For instance, one technology professional who was a participant in the project explained that the whole emancipatory participatory process was new to them and that they felt reticent to participate at first.

In particular, this participant said that they had no model or approach that they could build on when they first attended the London sessions, which were the first sessions to be held. Although the professional said that they found this experience challenging, they also found it positive, they developed resilience through its processes, and they learned issues about different access preferences and disabilities they had not worked with before. This professional described the whole experience as highly enriching. Similarly, another technology partner said that the ARCHES project had changed their understanding of how technology could be inclusive through its design process rather than a simplistic idea of its interface alone, what he referred to as an adaptive interface.

> I think for me personally it opened a little more even the horizon of what is an inclusive technology versus an adaptive technology. And where it's inclusive, more inclusive led the best option, or where is it better to adapt to specific needs of specific people, and why can that also mean inclusion.

However, although a number of participants thought that ARCHES sessions would lead to changes, others were less optimistic and felt that step changes made by the project and the narrative of its sessions would be small. One museum professional, for example, was less-committal when answering the question and could not provide specific instances of change when answering the question, "Is ARCHES creating opportunities for social action?" Instead, they felt that the changes made by the museums and technology partners would be less perceptible than the rest of his group. "I think it will make a difference. Maybe the difference will be smaller than we expected. I don't know. I mean, but the important thing is that there is a difference."

Ethical validity

As with the analysis of catalytic validity, analysis of the ethical validity seemed to show that a degree of ethical validity could be observed throughout the course of the project, with a number of participants saying that they had felt as if they had been treated fairly. Significantly, the answers suggested that the project had been ethically run and developed by the museum professionals coordinating the groups. Furthermore, there also seemed to be a strong ontological correlation between an understanding of ethical validity and participatory, intersubjective, empathetic, and ethical validities.

For example, in one instance, a number of participants stated that they felt the project had been balanced, with their voices being heard during sessions. Elsewhere, participants stated that they felt that the majority of the participants had been treated equally, and the group sessions felt like a safe place to voice concerns and express themselves confidently. In particular, one participant stated that the project had respected participants' differences, tried to integrate everyone in a collaborative way, and the tools and technologies developed during the course of the sessions would be enriched by inputs from these different perspectives. Another participant from the same city, when asked whether they had been treated ethically, stated:

> Of course. Absolutely. . . . If not, I wouldn't be here [laughter] on one hand, of course, but I mean it's obvious. It's obvious . . . It's obvious because of their purpose of the project and it's obvious because of the people working and involved in the project.

Other participants with more significant access needs felt that the project had provided an opportunity to be honest about their feelings of inequality and allowed them to socialize more equally with participants with less significant needs. There was also a general feeling that everyone was listened to at some point during the sessions, and even when people were skeptical or cynical about the implementation of the project, they were allowed to express their feelings openly. However, despite these comments, there was a belief that the power that some participants held could challenge a sense of fairness. In particular, there was a concern by some participants that a few of their peers were being listened to more than others, and those who spoke more were being listened to inequitably. It was also felt that some participants who were shyer found it difficult to get their voice across, given the confidence of others. As one participant stated:

> Well, as in all groups there are people who voice their concerns more loudly than others. I think several people have already, not in a bad way, but [others] have been sitting back a bit more. . . . Yeah, that's part of the game so to say.

Empathic validity

As previously stated, during the interviews, perhaps one of the strongest elements of participation was the development of a sense of empathy during the course of the group sessions in the four different cities. Even when staff members or those with access preferences were critical of certain aspects of the project or felt frustrated about their technologies, they all seemed to have at least a sense of empathy for the access preferences of others. For example, one participant described a situation where a fellow participant with what they described as "a strong intellectual disability" found it initially stressful to attend or be heard during sessions. This problem was particularly acute as this participant had joined in the middle of the project, which they felt made it harder for him to bond with other members of the group of feel accepted by others. However, after different members of the group worked with this participant over a period of time and gave him increasingly more responsibility, they noticed the participant grew in confidence. Eventually, this participant found themselves putting their opinions across and was even given the opportunity to make public presentations.

> This guy, this person was so closed, so shy, so introspective the very first day. And, last week when we did the intermediary middle term presentation of the project, he made a presentation on top of the stage and he was brilliant. And, now you see him interacting with the rest of the group, putting his opinion on top of the table, making his arguments, discussing, so it's brilliant.

However, there was empathy not only for different access preferences but also for the responsibility and roles of museum professionals and technology developers during the course of ARCHES's sessions. In particular, it was observed that discussing each other's roles and experiences during the sessions had helped each participant understand the nature of museum and technology roles and responsibilities, and the difficulty in providing their services. It also appeared to provide an insight into the difficulties of engaging with the museum as a person with access needs and disabilities.

Another theme raised on numerous occasions was the necessity of longevity as a catalyst for generating empathy and a feeling of fairness among the participants. For example, following what can be described as uneasy exchanges during the early sessions between museum professionals and those who were recruited for their access preferences, it was felt by some that participants now understood each other's needs more clearly as a result of these exchanges. In this way, even tensions made it more likely to develop a sense of resilience among participants of all types given the extended passage of time the project provided. As one participant said:

> I think I know what blind people need. But of course, now without all the other disabilities, so yes, this increased empathy in our case. But yeah, for the whole project I think just working together should increase this in any case, and I think this part worked quite well in ARCHES. Working two years together simply has to increase it.

A number of other participants felt that working on many of the tasks had helped them gain a sense of empathy of others' access preferences and the general needs of other museum visitors. Although this was not a focus of the tests and was not a point that was considered in the original test designs, there was a belief that empathy occurred "organically," as a process of education. For example, one participant stated that the use of technologies developed during ARCHES had enabled them to understand that technologies could not simply be labeled as accessible by a single category of disability, such as blindness and deafness. Moreover, during the course of the project, this participant said that they had realized that technologies cannot be labeled as inclusive simply by being designed with the intention of providing access:

> Oh yeah, I've learned a lot. I've learned that access is many things. And yeah, I've learned that it is very much down to the individual and cannot be labelled as easily. I mean, we've had this conversation when we started, we never, I never wanted to put people into, all blind people are the same. But it did, yeah those conversations have helped a lot.

However, for a number of participants, the development of empathy was occasionally tempered by a feeling that having empathy for another participant's access preferences could not help fully understand the whole of that person's needs, or what it was like to actually have another access preference. For example, one participant stated that although the tests and exercises they had developed and undertaken during the sessions had provided a theoretical understanding of other participants' needs and preferences, he was not confident that his capacity to work with all other participants in his sessions had improved in a practical way:

> OK yeah, [he understands other's preferences] in a theoretical way, yes, but he is not sure if he could help a blind person or a person that can't hear so well if he really has to, yeah.

Problems that arose through participation and the development of further validities

During the emancipatory participatory sessions, the problems that arose and the respective tensions they created became a meta-focus of the research, and thus data were termed tensions-data. During analysis of this tensions-data, it was also found that several tensions went beyond the original evaluation's validities and allowed the participants to develop a better understanding of unique participatory practices that could inform future as well as current practices. What now follows is the result of this analysis.

Tensions caused during participatory practice

The most observable tensions that were observed during the project often related to the roles that each participant had or perceived that they had during the project. Within this broader issue, subissues of the ambiguity of the *role of the participant*, issues of power caused by these roles and the underlying tensions that underpinned the formation, practice, and delivery of the results arose during a number of the group sessions in all four cities. Subsequently, during the early period of the project, *partner participant* and the *volunteer participant* roles seemed to emerge, each bringing their own pervasive cultures to the project, with these cultures causing their own interlacing tensions.

As we discussed earlier, these partner participants were, by their nature, professional participants and their roles related to the skills and knowledge they brought with them to the project, the individual funding they received, and the research targets and technologies that they were responsible for. The subroles of the partner participants were identifiably the individual professions and professional cultures that each person brought with them to the project. These subroles often brought their own communication and professional issues, and as one partner stated of the early development of the project:

> There have been problems in ARCHES I think, I believe that and probably it has been a problem not just of the companies, [but] for everyone. We haven't explained ourselves probably well, the universities and the museums maybe we needed to talk more with the companies and explain how we work. Also then we kept inviting them to the groups and they never came, that was important to understand how we work. . . . Probably the technological companies have a way to work that's not participatory at all, so it doesn't help. Usually we don't have a participatory way of working either so we handled that ourselves.

By contrast, the volunteer participants were either those that had been invited to be members of the group or those participants who had a voluntary role in supporting, advocating for, or guiding other participants during the sessions. In some circumstances, volunteers were also the carers of volunteer participants within the groups—including parents or other family members—although this latter subrole did not cause considerable tensions during the project. However, there were observable tensions between those volunteer participants who came with their own previous skills and knowledge, either as an advocate for a disability rights groups or through a prior professional or voluntary advisor role, and those who had not had these roles previously. Consequently, in the voluntary group, two further significant subgroups emerged, the *novice volunteer*, who had not participated in such projects before, and the *experienced volunteer*, who had.

A breakdown of the tensions that caused the problems

The most significant tensions generated within the project were between those who had different roles within the emancipatory participatory groups and those who were participants, partners, and part of a broader project—that is to say, those participants who were largely partners and voluntary participants, and those participants who had the subroles such as an engineer or, largely speaking, academic. For example, it was observed that some volunteer participants often became dependent on individual professional participants in the group, while some participants with more significant access preferences chose to sit next to selected professional participants (Hayhoe et al. 2018). These professional participants were then asked to scribe or read for them, and a form of dependency on this relationship between nonpartner participant and partner participant thus developed. Such relationships could be long running, with participants asking to sit next to professional participants in all the sessions, or nonpartner participants asking if these partner participants would be available or not. Although these dependent relationships did not appear to prevent participation by each group of participants, there were occasional complaints of favoritism by other nonpartner participants. Furthermore, there was a perception by some nonpartner participants of undue emphasis being placed on the voice of these "favored" nonpartner participants. These tensions then often led to nonpartner participants questioning the power imbalance during the sessions and in the project as a whole.

Similar power imbalances were also perceived among the partner participants during the development of technologies, with the economic culture of the technology companies and the lack of power of the museums being cited as a complicating factor during the project. For example, Participant A felt that tensions were caused by each partner thinking of themselves as an agent for their institution or class of institution, which they referred to as the technology company agent or the museum agent. Thus, because ARCHES largely existed within and was designed to provide facilities for museums, Participant A felt that the separate internal motivations of each partner necessarily complicated the evolution of the development of inclusive practices. This agency, he asserted, seemed to be largely motivated by traditional practices that agents brought with them and their understanding of the aims of ARCHES as they aligned with their own individual aims. This led Participant A to feel that the individual agencies' expectations (what he referred to as baggage that partners brought with them to the project) caused friction when each agent was seen to impose these expectations on synergistic relationships within the project. As he said:

> This economic outcome is complicating too much the relationship ... with the technology companies. More even than the relationship that the museum and the university has, because, and this is really frustrating for us to see that we become as clients, but not clients in a way that we can decide, as clients, you know free clients and in a free market. But like when you receive funding and you are obliged to work with someone.

Furthermore, a number of participants noticed a power imbalance between partners that was caused by a lack of experience, knowledge, and expertise in certain key areas of the project's outputs. For instance, it was observed that some museum professionals would not think of themselves as researchers and thus able to contribute as much to the technological development of the project as academics or technology professionals did. In particular, Participant B said that they felt their main role was to simply provide feedback to the technology companies about topics such as usability or technical problems. This perception, Participant B said, was reinforced in the wording of the research contract and its assignment of specific roles during the project, an issue that was designed to provide responsibility for each element of the project.

INTERVIEWER: You don't see yourself as part of the research or as a [researcher] yourself?
RESPONDENT: To an extent yes, in maybe the feedback that I gave or with some of the things which concerned the technology and apps and games but nothing like [the university researchers]. I think I was more of a facilitator than anything else and I think that was kind of what the contract was. When you read through the contract it does say that museums are more there just to facilitate the sessions and to make sure that everything runs smoothly and okay and that we're there for the groups. But research, when I'm asked to do something, I will do it but I'm not a researcher.

Within the museum's participatory groups, there were also tensions generated within the partner institutions themselves, with all ARCHES partners having to function within strict curatorial and management practices and policies. For instance, it was observed that museum policies led museum professionals involved in ARCHES to worry that they were being pulled between their roles as advocates and facilitators of participation yet at the

A large museums-based project   63

same time having to work within their own institutional culture. Consequently, some partner museums found it difficult to implement the planned innovations of technology, information, and practice that technology companies often require separately from the role they held in ARCHES. For example, one of the cornerstones of access for people with stronger learning access needs is the use of Easy Read texts, that is to say the use of simple grammatical structures and vocabulary in short vignettes that presented small "chunks" of knowledge. Although the data collected during the sessions were enthusiastic about the use of these texts throughout the museums involved in ARCHES, some museum professionals found it difficult to convince their curatorial staff that this text should be available in *all* circumstances. As Participant C stated:

> I still don't think our curators, for example, are convinced yet that all text labels should be in Easy Read. I think they'd be happy about having easy read labels available but not in a universal design principle.

Another power imbalance between the museum partners and the technology and academic partners was the role that the institutions had in drafting the original proposal and the funding contract. In particular, many of the museum professionals felt that ARCHES was too often driven by technological development and academic research rather museum-based inclusion or access *supported* by new and emerging technologies. In addition, a number of museum professionals felt that many of the research decisions were taken at the beginning of the research, particularly during the London-based sessions, and that these decisions and strategies were then imposed on the continental museums. For instance, Participant D from Spain stated that the communication rules that were developed in London and then transferred to the other museums took little account of the cultural differences or diversity of the participants or the need for different communication traditions. For some museum partners, it was even felt to be insulting that their emancipatory participatory groups could be adjudged to need lessons in discussion and empathy for their diverse and often skilled participants. As Participant D stated:

> I think that in this negotiation the university and technological companies were the ones to decide [the] objectives and not the museums, or not at least all the museums who were inside the project. Us intervening in the second phase of the project, it prevented us from having more impact and I think honestly maybe now I am throwing flowers to myself. The pilot group in London has done something that was not relevant for us apart from the practical issues and they were telling us

things like you should make the communication rules. We work with groups, there is no way a group is going to work between each other if they don't have communication rules.

Concluding discussion—addressing the tensions within the group

Overall, there was no single strategy that could address all the tensions that arose. This was largely because the same tensions could have different contexts in different emancipatory participatory groups and different national and professional cultures. Furthermore, some tensions, such as partners having to function within strict curatorial and management practices and policies, were unresolvable during ARCHES, as they largely existed outside the project's remit. Subsequently, there also needed to be a pragmatic approach to evaluating and reacting to what could be achieved within the time provided. However, over the course of the project, the participants reflected on these tensions, discussed them openly in partner meetings and emancipatory participatory groups, and fed back through emails and social media. Furthermore, what we learnt from working with different national, institutional, and professional cultures and diverse partner participants compensated at least in part the tensions caused by differing points of view. For instance, Participant D, who prior to ARCHES had worked in various roles and lived in numerous jurisdictions stated:

> Well I guess [that] in the general meetings it's very often that, it's kind of conversation. Many things that are not even easy to grasp or to describe but I've worked in the three [countries], I've lived in the cultural ambiance, so I more or less know how people tick and what you need. And I very often, even also the [Partner E, Country A], I very often had to take them aside . . . I guess [Country A] people and the museums, so corporates and the [City A] museums especially sometimes had some communication problems or something like this. And so, I took the guy aside, and took him to another room and offered my help to solve the problem.

It also helped that the project took place over a relatively long period as many of the tensions faced took time to resolve. This information sharing and the chance to experiment with solutions over the course of ARCHES allowed good practice to emerge and a common approach to reducing tensions to evolve. Having three years to work on the project also gave participants the freedom to reflect and evolve on their roles within the group, and as a result, tensions became less frequent by the end of the project. Consequently, the sessions generally speaking became less complex and more open to differing roles, interlinking paces of development and levels of participation, and as a result, the participants often grew less timid and contributed more. As Participant E stated:

> I think it's quite complex, there are different layers around accessibility and around the technology and around the group dynamics. I've actually found that the credibility of it, the meaningfulness of it has increased, and in particular in terms of I think there's been a growing focus and a growing success in really handing over the dynamic to the group much more. I think the group were quite passive 18 months [ago] in relation to where we are now and as someone who was sitting and watching and dipping in and out of different conversations with different people, I just get this sense of a coherence and for me . . . I think personally the whole way in which you have such a different range of access needs for a group to gel as a group, I think has really moved on and that for me has been the key point of credibility.

Eventually, three strong, reliable meta-themes emerged that helped to relieve the most stubborn, addressable tensions. These themes were (1) *reflexivity*, that is to say, the ability of the participants to reflect on the tensions as they arose and the flexibility to develop common strategies that could overcome them; (2) *learning*, the ability of the project to learn about new situations and concepts as they arose, and more importantly the ability and willingness to learn about other professionals, access needs, and national cultures during practice; (3) *communication*, the ability of the project to develop and continually adapt lines of communication, to discuss tensions, and to address issues in a broad network. For example, Participant F found that learning about inclusive technology and "buying into" an emancipatory paradigm helped him better understand what the emancipatory participatory groups wanted. Subsequently, as a result of his learning experience, he found he could adapt the technology that he was responsible for developing and take a different view on access needs. As he stated:

> I think for me personally it opened a little more even the horizon of what is an inclusive technology versus an adaptive technology. And where it's inclusive, more inclusive led the best option, or where is it better to adapt to specific needs of specific people, and why can that also mean inclusion.

Therefore, at least three more validities based on the underlying themes that helped to resolve tensions arose through the sessions for future development, planning, practice, and evaluation of projects. These validities are as follows:

- *Reflexive validity*—Whether participants can respond to lessons learnt from the project, either on a personal level or as incentive to develop their own projects. This validity also asks participants to consider whether there has been professional development that allows them to develop their own career paths or other individual goals through participation if needed.
- *Learning validity*—Whether the project has a significant scope as a learning project, and allows participants to learn new skills and knowledge during participatory practice. This validity should not only allow participants to learn about each other's professions and skills but also show participants how their contributions can develop future research, their careers, their role as an expert, and the sustainability of emancipatory participatory research.
- *Communication validity*—Whether the project develops a web of communication and allows participants to communicate with each other on an equal level no matter where their location, educational level, or ability to articulate themselves. This validity should also address power imbalances and tensions within the emancipatory participatory sessions and partner meetings, and act in-concert with the learning validity to make participants feel that they are valued equally throughout the process of participation.

5 Conclusion

Through this book, we have wanted to develop disability research to benefit people with disabilities and explore what that means from a theoretical and practical perspective. Doing so has allowed us to engage with, and develop an argument for, a contemporary and ongoing debate in disability studies and the social sciences in general. Hence, it is our belief that all disability research in the social sciences should attempt to be emancipatory.

This emancipatory paradigm assumes a Foucauldian conceptualization of emancipation as ongoing individual and societal development to resist political, cultural, and material circumstances. It also acknowledges that these processes are necessary in the current context of disability because ongoing political, cultural, and material circumstances frequently lead to inequality.

The exploration of the nature of emancipation and emancipatory research in disability in this book is not exhaustive, because it has been limited by its purpose as a focused introductory text. As such, intersections between the emancipation of disabled people and factors such as non-Western cultural contexts, race and ethnicity, and sexuality have not been investigated as they do not fall inside our current remit and objectives, although these remain important to a general debate. In addition, the analyses of the benefits and weaknesses of research designs and practices are of necessity brief as each could fill a much more comprehensive book on their own.

So, what does our model of emancipatory participatory methodology look like in practice?

By consulting and involving people with disabilities in gathering knowledge that will ultimately lead to their own inclusion, and by enabling participants to dictate their own *sense of inclusion* (Hayhoe 2019), Foucault's

68 Conclusion

concept of resistance is slowly becoming genuine. This has not only led to more practical and effective educational, cultural, and technological access but also acted as a catalyst for further social and cultural action and to the development of skills that enable self-advocacy and increased employment.

Now, institutions internationally are starting participatory groups not only in single research projects but they are also developing permanent, purposive, and evolving participatory groups that not only develop knowledge but also evaluate and propose inclusive policies on an ongoing basis. Over the course of the life of these groups, participants not only challenge the institution but also often challenge what we understand about disability and ability: they challenge the use of technologies, they question institutional hierarchies and the favoring of individuals or groups over others, they interrogate research methodologies and educational policies and practices, and importantly they contest their own perceptions of each other.

Through its work, emancipatory participatory research and practice has also led to the development of new models of knowledge-exchange and a research methodology based on participatory spaces, ethical practices developed by participants themselves, and models of cross-cultural participation. These models are not only practical tools for educational institutions, but they are also research instruments providing a method of evaluating future participation and access and drawing a road map for policy making.

Furthermore, emancipatory participatory research has broken down previous boundaries of research cooperation, by joining educational, technological, and support professionals in partnership with people with a range of disabilities and other access preferences. Perhaps equally important, this new form of research has shown that participation can transcend institutional and political borders and contribute to a greater trans-cultural understanding of inclusion and access, as well as new forms of acknowledging exclusion and inequality.

However, it has to be conceded that the practices and experiences of working together in participatory groups have led to tensions: tensions between participatory groups and institutional managers; tensions between researchers and participants with disabilities and access needs; access between institutions wanting to drive forward an understanding of inclusion and more traditional institutions; tensions between a carefully manufactured image of inclusion and messy reality; tensions between people with different forms of disabilities; and tensions between the egos of different participants. This suggests that the emancipatory paradigm on which this practice is based needs to evolve further and to consider these intersections and personal psychologies that drive tensions.

Many of these tensions have been outlined in the case studies in the previous two chapters. However, although these tensions make emancipatory

Conclusion 69

participatory research difficult, they have also served to improve them and served as lessons for participants and researchers to develop a sense of resilience, communication, and reflective learning in their practice. Importantly, as emancipatory participatory research evolves further into a new maturing methodology, these tensions need to be developed to increase empathy between all participants based on their roles as researchers, managers, technologists, supporters, teachers, visitors, and students. Hence, it is also hoped that this book has inspired its readers to become involved in this process of questioning, challenging, and developing emancipatory participatory research further.

References

Axel, E., 2018. Art Beyond Sight: A Way Forward. *Keynote Presentation, Developing a Community of Practice through Inclusive Capital Symposium*. University of Bath, Bath, Somerset, UK – March.
Bancroft Library, 2004. *Introduction: The Independent Living Movement* [Online]. Available from: http://bancroft.berkeley.edu/collections/drilm/introduction.html [Accessed 5/10/2018].
Barnes, C., 2003. What a Difference a Decade Makes: Reflections on Doing "Emancipatory" Disability Research. *Disability & Society*, 18, pp. 3–17.
Barnes, C. and Mercer, G., 2003. *Disability*. Cambridge, UK: Polity Press.
Barnes, C. and Mercer, G., 2010. *Exploring Disability: A Sociological Introduction* (2nd ed.). Cambridge, UK: Polity Press.
Barton, J. D., 2018a. *A Critical Thematic Exploration of the Epistemologies of Disability Found within the Policies and Outputs of the Higher Education Academy (HEA) and the Higher Education Funding Council for England (HEFCE)*. Bath, UK: University of Bath.
Barton, J. D., 2018b. *Independent Research Essay: Exploring Emancipatory Disability Research in the Social Sciences* [Unpublished]. Assignment (MRes). 2017–18 MRes Health and Wellbeing, University of Bath.
BSA, 2017. *BSA Statement of Ethical Practice*. Durham, UK: BSA Publications.
Campbell, F. K., 2009. *Contours of Ableism: The Production of Disability and Abledness*. Basingstoke, UK: Palgrave Macmillan.
Cohen, L., Manion, L. and Morrison, K., 2005. *Research Methods in Education* (5th ed.). New York: Routledge Falmer.
Coole, D., 2015. Emancipation as a Three-Dimensional Process for the Twenty-First Century. *Hypatia*, 30(3), pp. 530–546.
Danieli, A. and Woodhams, C., 2005. Emancipatory Research Methodology and Disability: A Critique. *International Journal of Social Research Methodology*, 8(4), pp. 281–297.
Devlin, R. F. and Pothier, D., 2006. *Critical Disability Theory: Essays in Philosophy, Politics, Policy, and Law*. Vancouver, Canada: University of British Columbia Press.
Durham, J., Brolan, C. E. and Mukandi, B., 2014. The Convention on the Rights of Persons with Disabilities: A Foundation for Ethical Disability and Health

References

Research in Developing Countries. *American Journal of Public Health*, 104(11), pp. 2037–2044.

Ewens, D., Nightingale, C., Law, C., Challenger, S. and Byford, K., 2011. *Enabling Equality: Furthering Disability Equality for Staff in Higher Education* [Online]. Available from: www.ecu.ac.uk/wp-content/uploads/external/enabling-equality-furthering-disability-equality-for-staff-in-HE.pdf [Accessed 5/10/2018].

Fairclough, N., 2001. *Language and Power* (2nd ed.). Essex: Pearson Education Limited.

Finlay, L. and Gough, B., 2003. *Reflexivity: A Practical Guide for Researchers in Health and Social Sciences*. Oxford, UK: Blackwell Science.

Foucault, M., 1983. The Subject and Power. In: H. Dreyfus and P. Rabinow (eds.), *Michel Foucault: Beyond Structuralism and Hermeneutics*. Chicago: University of Chicago Press.

Foucault, M., 1988. Technologies of the Self. In: L. H. Martin, H. Gutman and P. H. Hutton (eds.), *Technologies of the Self: A Seminar with Michel Foucault*. Amherst: University of Massachusetts Press, pp. 16–49.

Foucault M., 1997. The Ethics of concern for self as a practice of freedom. In: P. Rabinow (ed.), *Ethics, Subjectivity and Truth: The Essential Works of Michel Foucault 1958–1984. Vol. 1*. New Press, New York, NY.

Gillham, B., 2005. *Research Interviewing: The Range of Techniques*. Maidenhead, UK: Open University Press.

Gustafson, D. L. and Brunger, F., 2014. Ethics, "Vulnerability," and Feminist Participatory Action Research with a Disability Community. *Qualitative Health Research*, 24(7), pp. 997–1005.

Harry, B. and Klingner, J., 2007. Discarding the Deficit Model. *Educational Leadership*, 64(5), p. 16.

Hayhoe, S., 2012. *Grounded Theory and Disability Studies: An Investigation into Legacies of Blindness*. New York: Cambria Press.

Hayhoe, S., 2019. *Cultural Heritage, Ageing, Disability and Identity: Practice, and the Development of Inclusive Capital*. Abingdon, UK: Routledge.

Hayhoe, S., 2020. *An Introduction to Grounded Methodology for Emerging Educational Researchers*. Abingdon, UK: Routledge.

Hayhoe, S., Garcia Carrizosa, H., Rix, J., Sheehy, K. and Seale, J., 2018. Accessible Resources for Cultural Heritage EcoSystems (ARCHES): Initial Observations from the Fieldwork. *Proceedings of the Educational Research Association of Singapore (ERAS) & Asia-Pacific Educational Research Association (APERA) International Conference*. Singapore, Singapore: Nanyang University.

Kant, I., 1991. An Answer to the Question: "What Is Enlightenment?" In: H. S. Reiss (ed.), H. B. Nesbit (Trans.), *Kant: Political Writings*. Cambridge, UK: Cambridge University Press.

Markula, P. and Silk, M., 2011. *Qualitative Research for Physical Culture*. London: Palgrave Macmillan.

Mietola, R., Miettinen, S. and Vehmas, S., 2017. Voiceless Subjects? Research Ethics and Persons with Profound Intellectual Disabilities. *International Journal of Social Research Methodology*, 20(3), pp. 263–274.

References

Miskovic, M. and Gabel, S. L., 2012. When Numbers Don't Add Up and Words Can't Explain: Challenges in Defining Disability in Higher Education. *International Journal of Multiple Research Approaches*, 6(3), pp. 233–245.

Morrissey, J., 2015. Regimes of Performance: Practices of the Normalised Self in the Neoliberal University. *British Journal of Sociology of Education*, 36(4), pp. 614–634.

Nencel, L., 2014. Situating Reflexivity: Voices, Positionalities and Representations in Feminist Ethnographic Texts. *Women's Studies International Forum*, 43, pp. 75–83.

Nuwagaba, E. L. and Rule, P., 2015. Navigating the Ethical Maze in Disability Research: Ethical Contestations in an African Context. *Disability & Society*, 30(2), pp. 255–269.

Oliver, M., 1992. Changing the Social Relations of Research Production. *Disability, Handicap, & Society*, 7, pp. 101–115.

Oliver, M., 1996. *Understanding Disability: From Theory to Practice*. London, UK: Macmillan.

Ostrove, J. M. and Rinaldi, J., 2013. Guest Editors' Introduction-Self-Reflection as Scholarly Praxis: Researcher Identity in Disability Studies. *Disability Studies Quarterly*, 33(2), p. E1.

Patton, M. Q., 2002. *Qualitative Research & Evaluative Methods* (3rd ed.). Thousand Oaks, CA: Sage.

Pezdek, K. and Rasiński, L., 2017. Between Exclusion and Emancipation: Foucault's Ethics and Disability. *Nursing Philosophy*, 18(2), p. E12131.

Priestley, M., Waddington, L. and Bessozi, C., 2010. Towards an Agenda for Disability Research in Europe: Learning from Disabled People's Organisations. *Disability & Society*, 25(6), pp. 731–746.

Rix, J., 2007. Labels of Opportunity: A Response to Carson and Rowley, Ethical Space. *The International Journal of Communication Ethics*, 4(3), pp. 25–28.

Rose, N., 1999. *Powers of Freedom: Reframing Political Thought*. Cambridge, UK: Cambridge University Press.

Shakespeare, T. and Watson, N., 2002. The Social Model of Disability: An Outdated Ideology? *Research in Social Science and Disability*, 2, pp. 9–28.

Shoukry, L., Sturm, C. and Galal-Edeen, G., 2015. Pre-MEGa: A Proposed Framework for the Design and Evaluation of Preschoolers' Mobile Educational Games. *Innovations and Advances in Computing, Informatics, Systems Sciences, Networking and Engineering*, 313, pp. 385–390.

Smith-Chandler, N. and Swart, E., 2014. In Their Own Voices: Methodological Considerations in Narrative Disability Research. *Qualitative Health Research*, 24(3), pp. 420–430.

Stone, E. and Priestley, M., 1996. Parasites, Pawns and Partners: Disability Research and the Role of Non-Disabled Researchers. *British Journal of Sociology*, 47, pp. 699–716.

Tremain, F., 2015. *Foucault and the Government of Disability* (2nd ed.). Ann Arbor, MI: University of Michigan Press.

Vaccaro, A., Kimball, E. W., Wells, R. S. and Ostiguy, B. J., 2014. Researching Students with Disabilities: The Importance of Critical Perspectives. *New Directions for Institutional Research*, 163, pp. 25–41.

Waterfield, B., Beagan, B. B. and Weinberg, M., 2018. Disabled Academics: A Case Study in Canadian Universities. *Disability & Society*, 33(3), pp. 327–348.

White, G. W., Simpson, J. L., Gonda, C., Ravesloot, C. and Coble, Z., 2010. Moving from Independence to Interdependence: A Conceptual Model for Better Understanding Community Participation of Centers for Independent Living Consumers. *Journal of Disability Policy Studies*, 20(4), pp. 233–240.

Williams, J. and Marvin, S., 2015. Impairment Effects as a Career Boundary: A Case Study of Disabled Academics. *Studies in Higher Education*, 40(1), pp. 123–141.

Wolbring, G., 2008. The Politics of Ableism. *Development*, 51, pp. 252–258.

Appendix

Preliminary contact email

Topic- MRes disability dissertation
Dear XXXX,

My name is Joe Barton and I am a (disabled) student on the MRes Health and Wellbeing course here at the University of Bath. My dissertation, which will be conducted over the summer, is based around exploring the experiences of academic staff who identify as disabled.

I was wondering if, when I reach the data collection phase, it would be possible to make your members aware of the project? To be clear I am not requesting contact details or any personal information, but perhaps I could send an information sheet to this email address or another method you deem appropriate. I hope that my research will be of interest and relevance to your members, and that some may be interested in being participants.

Please do email me if you have any questions and thank you for your time.

Kind regards,
Joe

Official contact email

Topic- disabled academic research project
Dear Sir/Madam,

You are receiving this email because you have indicated that you are interested in taking part in a research project exploring the experiences of disabled academics at the University of Bath. Attached are an information sheet, which provides all the details of the study and what being a participant would entail, and a consent form, which you will be asked to sign at the start of the research interview if you decide to participate in this study.

If you have any questions, please do not hesitate to email either myself (xxx@xxx.xxx) or this project's supervisor (Simon Hayhoe- xxx@xxx.xxx).

Kind regards,
Joe Barton

Index

Accessible Resources for Cultural Heritage EcoSystems (ARCHES) ix, 5, 40, 42–48, 51–52, 54–56, 58, 59, 60–64, 71
analysis 3–5, 6, 10–11, 14, 18–19, 20–21, 24, 25–26, 35, 43–44, 59
artwork(s) 44, 47, 50
Axel, E. 41, 70

Barnes, C. 2, 3, 8, 13, 14, 27, 70
Barton, J. 7, 9, 70, 74–75
British Sociological Association 10, 26
BSA *see* British Sociological Association

Campbell, F. K. 21, 70
Cohen, L. 19, 25, 70
Coole, D. 3, 4, 70

Danieli, A. 2, 3, 4, 7, 13, 25, 26, 70
data collection (methods) 1, 3, 4, 6, 7, 10, 12, 14–16, 18–19, 20, 22, 23–25, 46–48, 74
Devlin, R. F. 37, 70
Durham, J. 11, 27, 70

emancipation 1, 2, 3, 4, 7, 8, 26, 67
ethics 4, 9, 10, 13, 15, 27, 43
evaluation 4, 19, 38, 43, 46, 47, 48, 65
Ewens, D. 17, 21, 23, 34, 71
exclusion 2, 9, 10, 12, 13, 16, 18, 21, 23, 44, 68

Fairclough, N. 18, 25, 71
Finlay, L. 12, 27, 71
Foucault, M. 3, 4, 38, 71

Garcia Carrisoza, H. 40–66
Gustafson, D. L. 3, 71

Harry, B. 41, 71
Hayhoe, S. 10, 14, 43, 45, 61, 67, 71, 75
hypothesis 43, 44

interview(s) 21, 24, 27, 46, 74
invisible disability 4–5, 16, 20, 24, 28, 34

Kant, I. 3, 4, 71

learners 50
literature review 20, 22
London 5, 40, 42, 43, 45, 46, 56, 63, 71

Madrid 5, 40, 42, 43, 45
Markula, P. 6, 7, 9, 12, 13, 16, 19, 23, 25
Marxism 3
Mietola, R. 7, 25
Miskovic, M. 17, 23, 71
mobile technology 43, 44, 46
Morrissey, J. 36, 72

narrative 28, 53, 56
Nencel, L. 12, 27, 72
non-participant observation *see* observation
Nuwagaba, E. L. 7, 72

observation 45, 46
Oliver, M. 2, 3, 7, 8, 11, 13, 14, 26, 37, 72

ontology 6
Ostrove, J. M. 12, 27, 72

participant observation *see* observation
participatory methodology *see* participatory research / practice
participatory research / practice 1, 8, 11, 21, 40, 41, 42, 44, 45, 46, 48, 60, 66
Patton, M. Q. 15, 72
Pezdek, K. 3, 4, 72
philosophy 1, 2, 3, 4, 6, 8, 13, 19, 22
primary schools *see* school

qualitative 6, 7, 13, 14, 16, 18, 23, 38, 43
quantitative 6, 31, 32

Rix, J. 10, 40–66, 42, 45, 72
Rose, N. 37, 72

sampling 10, 15, 19, 43
school 17

Seale, J. 40–66
secondary school *see* school
self-emancipation *see* emancipation
Shakespeare, T. 3, 72
Sheehy, K. 40–66
Shoukry, L. 43, 72
Smith-Chandler, N. 19, 25, 72
Stone, E. 2, 3, 7, 72
systematic literature review *see* literature review

Tremain, F. 3, 4, 27, 37, 72

University 5, 13, 15, 17, 20–39, 42, 48, 52, 53

Vienna 5, 40, 42, 45, 50, 54

Waterfield, B. 17, 18, 21, 23, 38, 72
White, G. W. 9, 45, 73
Williams, J. 21, 36, 38, 73
Wolbring, G. 37, 73